continued from front fla
Mr Ashley

D1062137

Journey into
Silence

JACK
ASHLEY, M.P.

Journey into Silence

THE BODLEY HEAD
LONDON SYDNEY
TORONTO

To Pauline

319464

DA
591
.A92 A3
1973

© Jack Ashley 1973
ISBN 0 370 01384 0
Printed and bound in Great Britain for
The Bodley Head Ltd
9 Bow Street, London WC2E 7AL
by William Clowes & Sons Ltd, Beccles
Set in Monotype Ehrhardt
First published 1973
Reprinted 1973

CONTENTS

1

The Silence Falls

On the evening of December 1st, 1967, I attended a splendid dinner party at No. 1 Carlton Gardens, the official residence of the First Secretary of State, Michael Stewart. It was a serious as well as a social occasion for behind the splendour lay an exercise in power. Discussion at dinner, as at the conference which preceded it, could affect the lives of millions of people. As I listened intently to the experts planning radical changes in our social services I felt that the evening signified a new era for those in need in Britain—little realising that it was to mark the end of my normal life and the beginning of a remarkable new one.

I had become a Member of Parliament in 1966 and fifteen months later Michael Stewart invited me to be his Parliamentary Private Secretary. Although happy as a backbencher, I welcomed this opportunity because treading the corridors of government, reading Ministerial briefs and sitting in on vital policy conferences opened up a new world to me. I was beginning to appreciate the possibility of applying the theories I had long advocated—translating ideals into practical politics. Some commentators predicted that I would soon get Ministerial office and my private hopes were high.

There was only one small personal cloud on the horizon—my hearing.

My left eardrum had a perforation, due to an infection in childhood, and although this caused a partial loss of hearing it was not a significant one. But my right ear was failing despite three operations, known as stapedectomy. As the large rooms and halls of Parliament caused slight hearing difficulties, I decided to have a minor operation to repair the perforated left eardrum which, if successful, would give me virtually perfect hearing in one ear.

The decision was not made lightly, because my hearing functioned reasonably well and I did not believe that slight deafness would be a major barrier to a political career. I deliberated for some time but the surgeon's confident prediction of the outcome swayed me. It was a *minor* operation, improved hearing was virtually assured, and the risk of deterioration—even slight—was described as 'one per cent'. I was to put myself in the surgeon's hands the day after the Carlton Gardens dinner party.

One of the guests at the dinner was G. D. N. Worswick, the Director of the National Institute of Economic and Social Research. Wearing a large National Health hearing aid he was able to discuss deafness without inhibition or embarrassment and I noticed with admiration, and some amusement, how he unclipped the microphone from his breast pocket during dinner and placed it prominently in the middle of the table to facilitate conversation with the people opposite. He told me that he had undergone an operation which had seriously damaged his hearing though, fortunately, not destroyed it.

The day before the operation I had a mildly sore throat and because I was uneasy I told the surgeon and the anaesthetist. The surgeon's response was that he would make sure I had good antibiotic cover. The anaesthetist, who examined my throat, said: 'It's no reason why I shouldn't give you an anaesthetic.' I felt reassured, yet the precise nature of his reply raised a disturbing question. Was it a calculated evasion of comment on the desirability of an operation—or simply the straightforward response of a man who habitually restricted himself to speaking within the limited field in which he was qualified?

The following day I had the operation and immediately afterwards my hearing was very low. I comforted myself with the thought that the dressings would be mainly responsible, but I was sufficiently disturbed to ask the surgeon if he had performed a more serious operation than the repair of the eardrum; he told me he had not and that the dressing was reducing my hearing. His attitude was reassuring, yet I was vaguely aware for the first time that an event of profound significance in my life had occurred. I was not deeply worried but a suspicion grew which was never to be dispelled.

During the evening I developed a heavy cold which seemed more feverish than any I had ever known. When the surgeon came the following day he told me that he was ordering more antibiotic injections. Although I was not disconsolate, I was uncomfortable with the cold, and tense because my hearing was so low. Michael Stewart kindly offered to visit me but I declined because I felt the difficulties of understanding him might be embarrassing. My wife, Pauline, had to speak slowly and clearly before I could follow her;

[8]

she was very concerned about my deafness despite the confidence of the surgeon. He told me that there was nothing to worry about, my hearing would be all right and I could go home after a few days. When I went it was with grave misgivings.

It was soon obvious that something had gone badly wrong. I was ill, weak and deaf, unable to hear without the help of a borrowed hearing aid; even then voices sounded like vague mumbles, limiting my comprehension of speech. Each time Pauline telephoned the surgeon he was reassuring, but he agreed that we should visit him. He diagnosed a new infection but took no further action since he thought the slow-acting antibiotics I had already been given would be sufficient. On our return visit a few days later he was obviously surprised that my hearing was still very low, and this time he prescribed new antibiotics. The infection would clear up, the surgeon assured us; he was going abroad for three weeks and he expected my hearing to be normal when he returned. In the meantime I was to take the antibiotics and, he said, it would be all right for me to travel to my home town of Widnes in Lancashire for Christmas.

I travelled alone by train, Pauline and our three children following by car. My thirteen-year-old eldest daughter, Jacqueline, was disturbed by my deafness but assumed that it would be cured before Christmas; Jane, our nine-year-old daughter, unquestioningly accepted our assurance that it was a temporary difficulty which would soon be resolved, while Caroline, eighteen months old, was blissfully unaware of the problem. Despite the lurking doubts we hoped to enjoy our usual family reunion with my mother, my sisters and their families—but my confidence had begun to waver. The operation had undoubtedly failed but was it to become a disaster? It bothered me that while the powerful hearing aid amplified the sound of voices, they were still incomprehensible. During the journey I switched off the hearing aid, trying to listen to the familiar clickety-click of the train speeding over the line. There was nothing but silence.

When I arrived, my mother and sisters were very worried. My mother had been deaf for many years and she could only manage by using a powerful hearing aid. Now my hearing was worse than hers and we did not know whether it would deteriorate further. The infection showed no sign of clearing up, so a few days before Christmas, with the London surgeon still abroad, Pauline and I visited a Liverpool hospital. I was examined by a young doctor of Chinese origin who was suffering from a heavy cold. I decided against joking with him about Asian flu and asked to see the head of the department, an ear, nose and throat consultant whom I had met some time ago. He was off duty but he kindly invited me to his home for an examination: for the first time since the operation my hearing was tested on an audiometer.

The results confirmed my worst fears. My right ear was dead and only a flicker of life remained in the left one. The most powerful hearing aid was useless for the dead ear and of little help to the other because the vital nerves were damaged and were failing to transform noise into meaningful sound. It was a bleak diagnosis and I felt the shadows falling on my life. But the consultant was cautiously hopeful that a little hearing might be restored, possibly just sufficient to enable me to continue as a Member of Parliament. He prescribed new treatment and made arrangements for me to contact him if necessary during the Christmas holiday. I hoped it would not be necessary, but took some telephone numbers as a precaution.

The next few festive days were not as happy as those we had regularly enjoyed for the past twenty years, but on Christmas Eve at our traditional gathering we carved a large turkey, distributed presents and sang Christmas carols. Christmas Day was charged with its own magic of happy children and a gay and intimate family. I was cheerful, for the new treatment was successfully bringing my hearing back and making speech comprehensible. But as I was still convalescent I went to bed to rest after Christmas dinner. Caroline, sleeping in her cot nearby, roused me with her crying when she awoke shortly afterwards. I was elated at being able to hear sounds again without a hearing aid. The whole family rejoiced because my fears had proved unjustified and the threat of deafness had receded. My eldest sister Helen said: 'Wouldn't it have been awful if your hearing hadn't come back?'

Our relief was short-lived. On Boxing Day, as I was watching Rugby on television after lunch, the words of the commentator became blurred and indistinct. Afterwards the family had tea together, but as the strain of trying to understand the conversation became too great I went upstairs to rest. Shortly afterwards Pauline came to see me, but when she spoke I could not hear her voice at all. My first reaction was that the borrowed hearing aid had failed, so she went downstairs and brought the powerful one my mother used. It was only when I tried it with the power full on and still could not hear Pauline's voice that the truth dawned on me. My hearing had gone.

I appreciated the potential consequences of the disaster immediately, yet I felt oddly cool and dispassionate about it. Perhaps it was due to the shock, or possibly I subconsciously assumed that my hearing would return. Yet I was aware of a growing, icy apprehension.

Pauline hurriedly telephoned the Liverpool consultant, arranging for me to enter hospital the following morning. The implications of deafness were ominous, as I reflected on them that night, but I refused to let my imagination roam too far; it may have been through fear or perhaps because I still had some hopes. I tried to invest medical science with an aura of infallibility I knew it did not possess; like a drowning man I clutched at an imaginary straw.

It was a grim journey to Liverpool with Pauline. For the first time driving together, we were unable to communicate except when she made brief notes as we stopped at traffic lights or in queues of vehicles. At the hospital it was no longer a question of having difficulty in understanding some people; it was impossible to understand anyone; the formalities of answering questions for admission had to be conducted by Pauline. I was afraid, angry and frustrated— and I knew I was powerless to do anything about it.

I was taken to a small, soundproof cubicle where a solemn-faced technician clamped a pair of earphones over my head and indicated that I should signal when I heard anything. Watching him adjusting the controls, I recognised a total contradiction in my attitude. I knew without doubt that my hearing had gone, yet I hoped that this complicated piece of machinery would magically produce some evidence to the contrary on which the doctors could build. The technician played his part perfectly. He was non-committally pleasant, but I felt instinctively that he regarded my case as hopeless, my hope as forlorn.

The consultant began an intensive course of treatment in a desperate attempt to retrieve some hearing. He asked the advice of other specialists and eventually decided on a comprehensive approach. I was given antibiotics, cortisone, pills to reduce the water supply in my body, pills to increase the circulation of my blood, and even whisky. I wondered whether the whisky was administered for psychological purposes, but apparently it had medicinal value, helping to stimulate the circulation of blood to the ears. Most of the pills and potions were administered every four hours and it was an odd experience to be wakened at 2 a.m. and 6 a.m. to be given a stiff dose of neat whisky. I came to hate it, but at that time I was prepared to swallow anything if it was going to help to restore my hearing.

Every morning the technician came to my bed with his mobile equipment, clipped earphones on my head, and tested my hearing: it was practically non-existent. Three or four crosses on the audiogram formed a tiny curve which only just fitted on to the bottom of the paper. I was still unable to hear speech even with a hearing aid but by banging a spoon on a table or a piece of china I could hear a vague blur of sound. I did this constantly, checking my hearing in the only way I could, until the nurses asked Pauline if there was anything wrong with me. I was making such a din that they probably thought the deafness had affected my mind.

The daily tests seemed to dominate my thoughts because I knew the results were of crucial importance. Sometimes the crosses on the chart would rise a little—occasionally another one would appear. These were occasions for rejoicing and soaring hopes; on other days, when the chart showed a loss, I was correspondingly gloomy. It was a desperate fight to retain normality, yet the whole procedure was conducted in a cool, clinical atmosphere, completely without obvious drama. Everything I did, and all the actions of the doctors and nurses, were conducted in a matter of fact way, but we all knew that success meant a return to an ordinary life and the resumption of my political career, while failure meant a lifetime of total silence.

Soon after entering the hospital I heard the Liverpool trams clanking and roaring outside but, remarkably enough, their screeching and groaning sounds did not vary with the changes recorded on the technician's equipment. The first time I was allowed out of bed I went to the window and looked out at the street. To my astonishment, there were no trams or tramlines; the clanking and roaring I could 'hear' were noises within my head. Known in the medical world as 'tinnitus', head noises are a profoundly distressing by-product of some forms of deafness and they are incurable; my experience then was the first dose of daily suffering which any victim endures throughout his life. Doctors and consultants are helpless, so I was faced with the prospect of living in the worst of both worlds, deprived of any meaningful sound yet denied the tranquillity which others imagine to be one of the tiny consolations of total deafness.

During those days of tension and anxiety it was Pauline who sustained me. Two of our daughters, Jacqueline and Jane, had returned to London to go back to school and were cared for by Pauline's mother and sister. Caroline, now twenty months old, stayed in Widnes. Every morning Pauline would dress and feed her, leave her with one of my sisters, and drive the twelve miles from Widnes to Liverpool. She always entered the ward radiating infectious optimism. The dying days of 1967 were bitterly cold and as she came in, rosy-cheeked and smiling, I always felt my spirits soar. She sat on my bed with pen and paper, conversing in this odd way as if it was the most natural thing in the world. She masked her misgivings with great courage, invariably interpreting the technician's results to my advantage. Thus my slender hopes were kept alive.

I knew that my mother and sisters Helen, Mary and Margaret, were deeply worried, anxiously awaiting news from Pauline every day. We are a close and loving family, and as I did not want to distress them I suggested they should not visit me for a little while until my hearing improved. But they came after a week, hiding their anxiety, and affectionately lifting my spirits.

My morale was also boosted robustly one day when the door was flung open and the massive figure of Bessie Braddock, the local, legendary MP, burst in. She was a great Parliamentary warrior who fought many battles for the people she represented and when she heard I was in hospital she simply turned up at my bedside and wrote me confident, reassuring notes. Her spontaneous gesture and attitude were a great tonic.

One morning, a few minutes after leaving with a cheerful wave, Pauline returned looking pale and shaken. She had slipped and fallen on the frozen snow outside and broken her wrist. While arrangements were being made to have it set and put in plaster she rested in a room close to mine. While I was with her I tried to be as cheerful as she had been with me. A broken wrist was no lifelong tragedy, yet I felt more upset than at any time since I entered hospital; when she went for treatment my spirits sank and I imagined all kinds of complications in her injury. But Pauline did not allow this setback to upset her, although it meant that she was now unable to drive from Widnes to Liverpool and had to wait in the cold for an inadequate and slow bus service. Yet she persisted in spending every day with me.

When we were together *she* looked like the invalid, with her arm in a sling. Gradually we began to notice a contrast in the attitude of the nurses to each of us; they were far more concerned about Pauline's injury than about my deafness. One disability was visible, the other was not, and this affected their attitude. We were able to laugh about this at the time but it was a foretaste of the future when some people were to treat me with near condescension if I failed to understand what they said.

A few days after Pauline broke her wrist a bigger blow fell. As I was shaving, I noticed that the normal faint buzzing of my electric razor, which I felt rather than heard, had vanished. It was an ominous moment. When the technician arrived for his tests I did not mention it but waited for his reaction. He usually took about fifteen minutes, but after one or two tests lasting only a few minutes he left hurriedly, returning shortly afterwards with the consultant, who completed the tests himself. There had been a serious setback and the little hearing that had returned during my stay in hospital had almost completely gone. Once more there were only the three crosses right at the bottom of the chart. Every known method was used until there was nothing more left to try. The suspense had ended, but with disastrous results, despite the dedicated skill of the consultant. He suggested that in the last resort lip-reading could make verbal communication possible. He advised me to return to Widnes and visit the hospital daily for tests.

I was deeply disappointed, but grateful to the consultant, who had been so helpful and done as much as anyone could. Before I left the hospital he gave me new hope with his explanation of the possibilities of lip-reading; he said that in two or three months speech could be understood quite well. Of course it was an overstatement because mastering lip-reading takes years and even then it is a poor substitute for hearing. Yet without his encouragement I would have despaired in the next few months. He made me feel that there was a mountain to be climbed and I resolved to climb it; otherwise I might never have coped with what was to follow.

I left hospital in a car driven by one of my brothers-in-law who chatted to Pauline on the journey. This apparently simple, natural scene provided one of the greatest shocks of my life. I was astounded to see them sharing a car with me yet having a conversation from which I was totally excluded. The hospital environment had insulated me against the reality which now had to be faced.

My spirits, already low, plummetted when I was unable to understand my mother and sisters at home. I was no longer the lively, jocular person they had always known; we all tried to pretend but we saw through each other's pretence. During the afternoon I went for a short walk with Pauline and it was the bleakest stroll of my life, for on that cold, gusty day in Widnes I was obsessed with the enshrouding silence now dominating my whole life. All rational thought was engulfed by powerful emotion and depression; the unthinkable was becoming a reality.

On one of my visits to the Liverpool hospital I was asked to try some powerful hearing equipment. This was the moment I had been waiting for and I entered the room apprehensively, accompanied by Pauline. The consultant and a technician adjusted the apparatus; the large headphones were again gently clamped over my ears. Pauline was given a microphone and began to speak to me. Even with the help of this powerful machine I could hear only a few unintelligible scratches of sound. The consultant was delighted I could hear anything at all, but I was bitterly disappointed that I could hear so little—although I tried to hide it to avoid hurting his feelings. I knew then that my tiny wisp of hearing was so slight that even with the most powerful hearing apparatus the human voice remained incomprehensible.

We stayed in Widnes for another few weeks, making frequent visits to the hospital, but there was no significant change in my hearing. Near the end of January we went back home to the children in London. Pauline's mother and sister, Barbara, had readily agreed to stay with Jacqueline and Jane while we were stranded in the North and we appreciated their kindness. Barbara stayed with us for some months longer, unobtrusively taking over many household chores despite the pressure of her own demanding job. With remarkable understanding the family quickly adapted to my deafness, speaking very slowly and clearly for me. Pauline constantly sought to instil a sense of proportion by emphasising the faculties I had retained. Yet we were two baffled people groping in an eerie situation, endlessly searching for a solution to an insoluble problem.

The operation had been a terrible mistake but the damage was done and my remaining option was to see if the London surgeon could repair it. The confident consultant I had seen before the operation was now a nervous doctor, looking very apprehensive. He did a hearing test on an old-fashioned machine lacking the precision of the Liverpool instruments. It failed entirely to register any wisp of sound, confirming once more that my hearing was gravely and, almost certainly, irretrievably damaged. But the consultant said he would prescribe a further course of treatment which, I was to discover later, consisted simply of daily injections of vitamin B.

When I asked about the chances of recovery he was non-committal; he was shortly going to the United States and would discuss my case with two doctors—'the best in the world at this kind of thing'. I was astonished at this sudden display of self-deprecation since he had never taken pains to conceal the fact that he was considered to be one of the leading ear, nose and throat consultants in Britain. In reply to my question 'Will I be able to hear sufficiently to remain a Member of Parliament?', he shook his head. Then he spoke one word. Of course I could not understand it, so he picked up a pad and wrote 'journalism'. After showing it to me he pulled the pad out of its case and pushed it back so that the word was erased. I felt I ought to be impressed by the trick and he obviously thought so too, but in fact I was amazed at the casual way he was dismissing the political career I valued so highly. He made it seem like his writing on the pad—now you see it, now you don't.

His discussions with the two leading doctors in the United States never took place. On his return he said that he had not seen them but would write; later he told me that he had received replies and only one of them had heard of a similar case. The information was as useless as his vitamin injections. In a last desperate hope that my hearing could be restored I made the usual round of other ear specialists but they were all as helpless as witch-doctors so far as my case was concerned. Some simply shrugged and gave encouraging smiles; others treated me as if I was a congenital idiot and discussed my condition with Pauline. 'How old is he?' one enquired. He spoke without moving his lips, like a ventriloquist. 'Why don't you ask him?' Pauline replied. 'And try speaking a little more clearly.'

The consultants did their best; some went to a lot of trouble, but their knowledge of deafness was limited and their knowledge of how to treat the deaf was lamentable. Pauline and I left every hospital with sinking hearts and a growing certainty that medical science had nothing to offer.

Would it be possible, by a crash course in lip-reading and the minute help of a hearing aid, to remain a Member of Parliament? Everything depended on my ability to communicate. The most powerful electronic aids were only of marginal value because the aural nerve was almost destroyed; nothing could magnify speech to more than a vague, indefinable blur to me. I had to learn to lip-read.

I was advised to go to the Institute of Further Education for the Deaf in London which was then housed in a large building with a gloomy atmosphere. The teaching staff were helpful, but most of the class were old and understandably slow. The tone and style of the tuition were geared accordingly. Some of the lessons were based on the presumed chit-chat of retired people—'Would you like one lump of sugar or two?' Sometimes they took the form of soundless half-completed proverbs which individual members of the class had to lip-read and complete—'A stitch in time . . .'. When I moved to more advanced classes the material was less banal but it was all a desperately depressing experience, and each day I walked from Goodge Street station to the Institute with a heavy heart.

On the journeys I read of the drama and excitement of Parliamentary debates. The main issues were consumer protection and immigration until Roy Jenkins, the Chancellor of the Exchequer, introduced his controversial Budget in the middle of March. Aiming to save a record £900 million, he increased taxes on drink, driving and smoking, to the inevitable howls of rage. I had a high regard for Jenkins and supported those policies; but I could only read about them in the newspapers as I trudged to my lip-reading classes. I felt even more isolated, frustrated and despondent.

At the classes two men stood out from the rest, helping to ease my gloom; one was a musician in his early twenties who had been totally deaf for about two years. He was an intelligent, sensitive man whose lip-reading standard was encouraging. Although he rarely smiled, I came to realise that, behind the strain of lip-reading, was a pleasant and even gay character. The other was a teacher in one of the advanced classes who managed to make the lessons interesting and avoided the excessively slow mouthing which was the usual practice of some of the other teachers.

[17]

I read every available book on the subject and found many of them old-fashioned and inadequate. The surprisingly large number of people who speak without any clear movement of their lips soon made me realise the limitations of lip-reading. Some consonants and vowels are scarcely visible, being formed by tongue movements often hidden by teeth and lips; beards and moustaches create more difficulties. Groups of consonants like p, b, m, or sh, ch, and j are indistinguishable, while short vowels are extremely hard to identify. Lip-reading, I found, was infinitely more difficult than learning a foreign language; the Liverpool consultant had only been encouraging me when he said that the skill could be achieved in a few months. Anyone trying to learn Chinese can at least theoretically master the language; but in lip-reading much of the 'language' is not available to be learned. I inevitably stumbled over the additional handicaps of regional variations of speech and I had to contend with the major problem of individual differences. Lip-reading is an art based on recognising slight visual clues and using them imaginatively. The mind has to register lip patterns while working like a computer to select the correct meaning from a vast number of possibilities. Lip-reading is immensely difficult, a grossly inadequate substitute for hearing; the miracle is that with all the difficulties it still works at all.

The pace of the classes was too slow for me so Pauline and I compiled a series of charts with every conceivable permutation of consonants and vowels. Every morning and afternoon I visited the wives of some of our friends, who would repeat words and sentences from the charts while I vainly tried to understand them. It was a desperately fatiguing business for me, and they must have found it oddly trying. I often wondered what the neighbours thought as they saw me regularly enter the houses of friendly wives, then depart weary and bleary-eyed after half an hour.

Two of our best friends, Peter and Jean Thorpe, who lived nearby, suggested I should have additional practice with them in the evenings. The three of us would stand in front of a mirror, trying to identify and compare the lip movements of some elusive vowel or consonant. I have since learned that a half-hour intensive session of learning to lip-read is enough to cause eye-strain and tax concentration but at that time I was doing up to six half-hours a day. With the combination of eye-strain, tinnitus, and the battering of my nervous system, I could feel myself ageing day by day. The

head-noises were painful and sometimes agonising. Their intensity
varied from day to day, and even during the day, but I was never
free from them. They created a ceaseless cacophony sometimes
bordering on bedlam.

I began to feel punch-drunk, sometimes despairing of ever understanding the silently moving lips, but with a hearing aid the minute
whisper of sound made many of the lip movements more meaningful. Occasionally I practised lip-reading without the aid, hoping to
improve more quickly, but it was extremely difficult; at that time
only the scratches of sound made the near-impossible possible.

Meanwhile I resigned as Parliamentary Private Secretary to
Michael Stewart. (Shortly after the operation I had offered him
my resignation, but he had refused to accept it.) When he was
suddenly re-appointed Foreign Secretary I knew I could never
fulfil my responsibilities to him. Accompanied by Pauline, I went
to No. 1 Carlton Gardens to hand him my resignation. It was our
first meeting since the splendid dinner party; this time it was a
quiet, personal occasion over a cup of tea. We were both sensitive
to the drastically changed circumstances and I shall never forget
the immense depth of understanding and unspoken affection he
showed. We seemed to have a tacit understanding that the words
we spoke to each other bore little relation to our feelings. He was
the first Member of Parliament I had met since I left hospital and
he fully understood the significance of my resignation as his PPS
and possibly my resignation from the House of Commons. Whether
it was our personal empathy, the peculiar circumstances, or both,
I don't know, but our meeting was a source of solace and encouragement to me at that difficult time.

Although I was virtually totally deaf, my other faculties were
unimpaired, but I did not know whether I should be able to use
them effectively in Parliament. After Easter, 1968, the final decision
could no longer be delayed; it was time for me to return to the
House to see whether I could continue or would have to resign.

The day I returned, Tuesday, April 23rd, was one of the most
testing and memorable of my life. For the past four months I had
been fighting to preserve my political career which hung precariously
by the most slender and delicate thread. If I succeeded, all the work,
concentration, eye-strain and weariness would have been worthwhile; I left for the Commons exhausted, bewildered, apprehensive
—but oddly hopeful.

[19]

As I walked through the Members' Lobby I was aware of curious eyes observing me. There was a warm welcome from many of my friends who looked at the hearing aid, with its long cord, obviously wondering how I would manage. But I did not stop to talk to any of them—I waved, walked into the Chamber, and sat down. Would I be able to understand the debate? I turned the powerful hearing aid to full volume; there were only vague but meaningless blurs of sound as each speaker made his point. I tried to lip-read, but the government speakers were sitting with their backs toward me and speakers from the Opposition side, whose lips I could see moving, were too far away for me to hear even the slightest sounds. I could follow very little indeed.

I left the Chamber, took a long, deep breath, and walked into the bar. It was the most embarrassing experience of my life. Three or four Members converged on me at once, shaking hands, slapping my back and welcoming my return. Others waved, and somebody handed me a glass of beer. After the affabilities someone asked me a question. I could neither hear nor lip-read him so I asked him to repeat it. He willingly repeated it but as I still could not understand him I asked him to repeat it again. Then I saw an expression that was to haunt me endlessly in the years ahead. It was one of total perplexity and embarrassment—he did not know how to deal with the situation. When he repeated the question again he was probably shouting, because out of the corner of my eye I could see nearly everyone in the room turn and watch us; but I was still unable to understand. Swift and meaningful glances were exchanged and by this time I was perspiring. I muttered apologies and hurriedly tried to finish the glass of beer as one of our colleagues, who had evidently had a few drinks, decided he would clarify the situation. He joined us and obviously bellowed at the top of his voice, but to me it sounded like the rustle of a leaf—and I could not lip-read him. I finished the drink, smiled all round, thanked them, and walked out.

By chance I met a colleague who was himself very hard of hearing; we went out on the terrace to talk but I found it almost impossible to follow anything he said. The only message he conveyed to me was that he was a very clear speaker and that if I could not understand him he regretfully felt I would not understand anyone. 'But don't leave immediately,' he said. 'Give it a few months before you resign.'

When he left me I sat alone on the terrace watching the Thames.

It looked bleak and cold. It was early evening and although I did not expect the river to be busy it seemed exceptionally still—and silent. I thought I had known despair, but now I felt a chill and deeper sadness, as if a part of me was dead. After a while I went back to the Chamber, where the debate was continuing, but as speakers made their points there was for me total and unbelievable silence. Each Member on his feet appeared to be miming. My last support, that vague buzz of sound which had come to mean so much, had vanished—perhaps obliterated by the last desperate use of the hearing aid. At that moment I felt in my heart that I had begun a lifetime of tomb-like silence. I took a final look around the Chamber before leaving for home and my family, and to prepare for my resignation from the House of Commons.

2

Childhood in Widnes

As a child I had no problem with my hearing. The Liverpool–London express trains thundered over the Mersey bridge a quarter of a mile from my home and the sound of their whistles fading in the distance seemed to trail a melancholy note in contrast to the lively, repetitive crack of shunted wagon-buffers in a nearby factory. At 7.30 every morning factory hooters shrieked and blared strident instructions. The note was urgent and demanding; yet when they signalled the working day's end at 5 p.m. they seemed oddly muted and resigned.

The industrial town of Widnes, on the banks of the Mersey, is an important centre of chemical production. As the factories were built, rows of small, terraced houses went up alongside. The neighbourhood was drab and uniform, without a blade of grass in sight. Smoke and fumes nearly always covered the area, making us as conscious of the direction of the wind as any sailor. The wind rarely cleared the air; different winds simply meant different smells. We were particularly conscious of those coming from the factory that stood at the end of our street and from the copper works that occupied the whole side of one nearby.

Industry dominated Widnes and despite some pleasant localities it was mainly a poor, working-class town. Men who were employed worked long hours at hard, dirty jobs. Those who were not were bored and demoralised; they spent their time in dole queues or on street corners. But hardship creates its own comradeship and the town's saving grace was a rich community spirit.

Number 34 Wellington Street, where I was born, was a decrepit slum house which had what we called a parlour, two bedrooms, kitchen and a tiny scullery. There was no bathroom and the lavatory was at the end of a small backyard. In this pathetically inadequate accommodation my parents, my two sisters and myself lived with my aunt's family of the same size. We had the parlour and front bedroom while they lived in the kitchen and the other bedroom. Both families cooked meals in the scullery and shared the lavatory. I was never conscious of feeling overcrowded when I was very young, though my parents must have felt it, with three children and only two rooms.

My father was a labourer, and later a night watchman, at Imperial Chemical Industries; I remember very little about him as he died of pneumonia at the early age of thirty-five when I was five years old. He was a quiet and devout Catholic who went regularly to early morning Mass even when seriously ill. Everyone seemed to have a high regard for him; from all accounts he was a generous man, though he had little to give. As a night watchman working for low pay, he must have found it soul-destroying to spend so many hours walking around a dark, stinking factory.

The gravity of his illness had been effectively concealed from us and his death came as a great shock. I remember being taken with my two sisters, Helen aged seven and Mary aged three, to a nearby sweet shop the day he died—'Your Dad's dead, come and have a bag of sweets,' said our aunt. The stab of fear and insecurity sank deeply. My mother was left to cope with three young children, and in the 1920s this was a very daunting prospect, especially as she had to manage on the miserable pension of twenty-one shillings a week for the whole family.

'Mam' was a small, quiet woman with soft, brown eyes reflecting a gentleness which remained quite unaffected by the vicissitudes of widowhood, poverty and the responsibility of bringing up a family in those mean days. It was astonishing that so gentle a person could command the courage she displayed throughout such years. Confronted with the danger that the family would be broken up when my father died, she took a job scrubbing floors at night and in the early morning in the ICI offices. It was tiring work and she came home totally exhausted. We often went to the end of the street to meet her. The sack she used as an apron was always soaking wet; I usually carried it and the feel of this rough, wet sacking was for me the symbol of her drudgery.

Even in those early days I was struck by people's attitudes to widows and their children. There is a gush of sympathy and everyone is helpful, but then, inevitably, people resume their normal lives, and the widow is left to fend for herself as best she can. I noticed the abundance of goodwill and the absence of practical assistance. As I grew older I saw what loneliness meant to my mother when other families in the street had husbands and fathers around.

The burden of rearing the family and being the sole breadwinner must have been crushing. She was sometimes physically sick with exhaustion but I never remember her complaining. We children were anxious to help and although there was very little we could do, we sometimes bought her a great luxury: she was fond of coconut iced cake, which was sold for a penny a slice. We used to buy her a slice out of whatever pocket money we had and hurry home eagerly with it, though we probably gained more pleasure from the giving than she did from the eating, particularly as she always shared it among us. The affection she lavished on us lightened the poverty of our lives, binding together our warm, close-knit family.

Our dependence on our mother was total and I always feared that if she were to die we would be sent to an orphanage. Everyone felt sorry for the local orphans who often played in a band at civic and social functions. Dressed alike in grey jerseys and dark short pants, they seemed robbed of their individuality but it never occurred to me that our shoddy clothes reflected an individuality which they would hardly envy. My feelings for my mother, although tinged with fear of the consequences if she were to die, were firmly based on a deep love for her as a person. Her rather shy affection, combined with a lively sense of fun, deeply enriched my life. Our relationship never changed and I always regarded her with deep and affectionate tenderness. She lived until she was 72 and today, years after her death, I think of her often and feel a brooding sense of profound and incomparable loss.

No doubt she was distressed by the conditions of our home. I accepted them because I was so young and I did not know anything different. We had no electricity and lived by gaslight which frequently faded. The shout 'the gas is going' was a signal for someone to jump to the cupboard where a few pennies were stored, and slot one into the meter. After the first flicker the gas faded quickly. If there were no pennies in stock, which was by no means unusual, the family groped around in darkness until a coin was found. Sometimes the light would not return after a penny had been put in the meter which meant that the gas pressure needed regulating. For some reason I never understood, filling a section of the meter with water usually solved the problem. But sometimes this did not work either, so we had to drain the water by unscrewing a stopper at the bottom and, the moment the light came on, replace the stopper quickly.

It was not simple to perform this operation, especially in darkness or candlelight, because the meter was cramped in a small cupboard on the floor. If we were slow in replacing the stopper the light soon went out again and the whole process had to be repeated. Sometimes the gas mantle would break, invariably after the shops were closed; this meant sitting in half light until bedtime. In the bedroom our only light was from a naked gas jet. I took it as part of the natural order of things, as did the rest of the family, but, as with everything else, it hardly made for gracious or easy living.

Poverty imposed its bleak discipline on our lives and we wasted nothing. We ate bread and margarine or sometimes bread and jam but never all three together. No jam jar was ever thrown out with the slightest trace of jam; I was so skilful at scraping a jar with a knife that it would be left completely transparent. Damp coal dust could prolong a fire for hours; cinders would double its burning time—I could tell by a glance at the ash pan below the grate how many cinders I would be able to sieve from the ashes with my fingers. Shoes with holes could have their life extended by inserting a piece of cardboard cut to the shape of the foot. I was careful to avoid puddles in the street, not to keep my shoes clean but to keep my feet dry.

The streets around us always seemed to be bustling with life. We played rugby in the street with a piece of sacking tied with string; one of my friends once suggested we should pool our Oxo coupons and get a real, leather football. I agreed, not thinking that I would be depriving my mother of whatever *she* was saving the coupons for. After months of patient saving we waited anxiously for the football to be delivered. I was not present when it arrived; my friends quickly organised a game in the street and by the time I got there a lorry had run over it and that was the end of that. We were back to the sacking tied with string and my mother had lost her gift coupons.

Soccer was not very fashionable with us though we played it occasionally with a small rubber ball or even a tin can—the tin was useful because it could also be thrown in other games. One of our favourites was 'bungout' in which one of us threw the can as far as he could and while another lad retrieved it we all hid. Sometimes when the can went through a window we stayed hidden for a long time.

As we were short of coins, our 'kick-off' was determined by the leader of one team cupping his hands to his face and moistening one with his tongue. The other team had to guess which hand was wet but a skilled observer would notice that one side of his opponent's lips was moist; this was usually, except with subtle double-thinkers, an infallible guide.

None of us owned a bicycle but somehow nearly everyone acquired a 'gooch'—an old bicycle frame minus wheels, pedals, chain and brakes. A pair of small wheels from an old perambulator could always be found and a six-inch nail served as the axle. With these home-made scooters we could achieve commendable speeds, though braking was hard on our shoes. These were our staple games though there were diverting fashions—tops and whips would come and go for no apparent reason and 'trundles', thin hoops of steel or thick bicycle wheels without spokes, would be ferried around with great dexterity. In nearly every case the competitive urge dominated; we would compete as readily with tops and whips as with trundles or our tied sacking.

One of our great luxuries was to visit the local cinema, the Picturedrome, on Saturday afternoons. We cheered the stars of the Westerns—Tom Mix, Hoot Gibson and Ken Maynard—and when the villain was creeping up on the hero we would bellow 'Look behind you, Ken'. If the hero was not so well known the shout would be respectfully amended to 'Look behind you, mister'. The film was always preceded by a local talent show and decisions were made on the basis of audience applause—grossly unfair, of course, as we were less concerned with merit than with cheering our friends.

My mother tried to pay for our cinema visits but sometimes, when she could not manage it, my friends and I would try to slip into a side door beneath the stage and surreptitiously emerge in the darkness of the cinema to join the audience. The ploy was not used very often; we kept it for days when we could not afford to pay. But eventually it was discovered and we were locked out. We resorted to another trick which was equally successful for a limited period: as the audience entered, the attendants would tear the tickets in half and throw them into a narrow, deep box. As crowds of youngsters pushed in, some untorn tickets were thrown into the box and we scooped out what we could as we left the hall. We sifted through them to find the untorn ones, which we used the following week. After a while this was also discovered and the attendants began sewing the used tickets on to a string.

The cinema was an escape to new worlds of adventure for children and adults. There were few opportunities to evade reality—or each other—because people lived so closely together in poor surroundings. In the streets, which were rarely deserted at any time, neighbours stood chatting in groups for hours on end; in summer they brought out their hard, wooden chairs to sit gossiping.

Outside a public house near the end of Wellington Street we waited every Saturday night at closing time to watch the inevitable arguments and occasional brawls. The fights were vigorous though they never appeared malevolent—people who had been fighting one Saturday night would be drinking together the next. Sometimes families bickered as they left the pub; one couple were particularly prone to loud, abusive language. Although they had four children and were very poor, both parents went to the pub every Saturday. One night after quarrelling all the way from the pub to their home, about a hundred yards away, they continued shouting for some time until the husband pushed his wife outside and locked the door. In her anger, and no doubt conscious of the spectators' amusement, she smashed the window with her shoe, but her hand went through the glass which cut an artery in her wrist; the farce turned to tragedy when she died a few days later. Her remorseful husband went to Mass every morning after her death and died himself not long afterwards from what the neighbours called a broken heart.

Another eccentric couple who lived a few houses away from us were an Irishman and his wife who could hardly have had more strongly contrasting characters. He was a violent man given to blasphemous fury at the drop of a pint. She was a kindly, sentimental woman, utterly devoted to their only daughter who was chronically sick. When the child died, her mother turned her room into a shrine and no one, not even her father, was allowed to touch or move anything in it. To raise money for the church, she held pathetic jumble sales in her backyard but she was so generous that she found it difficult to accept even a few coppers for the old clothes and trinkets on sale. 'Ah, go on, sure you can have it' she would say in a thick Irish brogue to someone who asked her the price of an old dress. Many years later, when I was the shop steward at a local factory, I worked with her husband, a great ally, who would curse the bosses with a blistering vehemence. Unfortunately he dealt out the same treatment to anyone who disagreed with him and during one strike I had to stop him physically attacking another worker who wanted to return to work. Characteristically he killed himself by cutting his own throat with an open razor; his wife lived to be a hundred and received a telegram of congratulation from the Queen.

Neighbours helped fill some of the gaps left by inadequate welfare provisions. One woman in particular specialised in helping the bereaved. When people died they were dressed in a shroud, laid out in their homes for a few days, then taken to church before burial. The laying-out was not a job to be undertaken by a deeply affected relative so this plump, kindly woman would always be called in to perform the necessary service. It was customary for relatives and friends, including children, to see the dead after they were laid out in their homes. Even though I was so young, I clearly remember being lifted up to see the face of my dead father.

During my childhood I saw many dead people in their houses when I went to pay my respects. The procedure was to visit the house, look at the body and kneel by it to pray for the soul of the departed. In retrospect, I don't know whether we made these visits out of curiosity, a desire to show respect, or simply an uncritical acceptance of a long-standing tradition; probably we were influenced by all these factors.

Our next door neighbours were a childless couple who were comfortably off because the husband had a regular job. We were friendly with them though we could not afford to share their pleasures—the most my mother could afford for a holiday was a day trip to Southport or New Brighton, across the river from Liverpool, which was twelve miles away. The neighbouring couple spent a week at Blackpool every year and when they returned we were regaled with descriptions of these odysseys; the sun was twice as warm as in Widnes, sands were golden, shows were magnificent and hotels luxurious; every meal was described in mouth-watering detail. What we were missing of life's real pleasures! As a result of these tactless tales to a deprived family I spent my childhood visualising Blackpool as Shangri-La—an illusion that was only dispelled by actually visiting the place years later.

In our circles, any man with a regular job was practically an aristocrat. Unemployment was a fact of life and the prime cause of the surrounding poverty. Idle groups loitering on the street corner were part of the daily scene; some were tempted to supplement their dole by irregular means—the most common was to steal coal from wagons in nearby sidings. To see a group of men moving off at twilight with old sacks and shovels simply meant to me that they would have a fire in their grate the following day whereas we might not. Some went further and sold the coal. My mother would not touch it, preferring to do without a fire. This was partly just her basic honesty—she was anxious that I should always keep to the straight and narrow—but also partly because she was afraid the men might be caught and implicate us. Occasionally they were caught by the police, but then the neighbours discussed their luck rather than their morals.

Some people tried to relieve poverty by gambling. At that time off-course betting was illegal but it did not stop people backing horses. Any chance of making easy money was eagerly grasped; tipsters often walked cockily down the street to encourage the triumph of hope over experience. They always had inside information and for threepence would write the names of two fleet-footed certainties on a small slip of paper. The buyer was enjoined to 'keep it to y'self' and having paid the money he was inclined to play along with the tipster's game.

Once in a while my mother bought the tips and when she opened them I always had a sense of confidential conspiracy. The horses were duly backed for 3d each though, of course, some mishap usually prevented their certain victory. Oddly enough, the tipsters were never unwelcome. Perhaps they gave the names of different horses to different people—so *somebody* won—or maybe they were eloquent and persuasive apologists for repeated failures. But throughout my childhood they enlivened Wellington Street, especially on big race days, raising hopes that the bookmaker was ripe for plucking.

Our bookmaker was the most smartly dressed man in the street —or rather at the back of our street—perhaps because he was never plucked. He was dapper, brisk and unfailingly friendly. He had a wooden leg which never seemed to trouble him or spoil his appearance; it emerged like the end of a crutch at the bottom of his trousers. As a child I somehow felt this must be better than two ordinary legs for a man who had to stand so long. He stood outside our back gate taking bets every racing day from twelve noon until 4.30 p.m. and paid out at 6 p.m. Between the houses, which were back to back, ran a long, narrow entry, and a slight bend in it, outside our gate, provided a niche for him. His lookout man, a cripple, crouched at the near end of the entry while the bookie took bets.

At six o'clock a small crowd would be waiting, and the book-maker was just as prompt in settling as in taking bets. He paid out quickly and efficiently from a huge pocketful of silver and copper coins. Though we rarely got more than a few coppers back, I learned to scan his long book upside down to spot the pseudonym 'E. A. Ash' my mother used; when my turn came I could point it out immediately to avoid delay. He worked quickly not only to satisfy impatient customers but because there was always the possibility of a police raid.

The raids occurred periodically but they were probably gestures, showing the flag rather than making a realistic attempt to catch him. If police approached from the far end of the entry 200 yards away, someone would spot them, whereas if they tried the near end just behind him, the lookout would give a loud, unashamed, almost hysterical whistle. The smart bookmaker would simply push our back gate open, walk into the lavatory and wait until the police had gone. If we wanted to go to the lavatory, we had to wait until he had left.

The other popular gamble was 'pitch and toss'. On a patch of spare ground near the local docks a crowd would gather to bet on whether two tossed pennies would turn up heads or tails. The betting money was casually thrown in heaps on the ground before the coins were tossed. I never played because my mother persuaded me that this was gambling by people who were heading for trouble. I did not question the moral distinction between this form of gambling and backing slow horses but took it for granted that players of pitch and toss would get their deserts. Surprisingly often they did so, because the police raids were dramatically successful. Dozens of men would be caught with their pennies down by intrepid police who either disguised themselves or hid in dirty wagons which were shunted nearby. When the names of the guilty appeared in the local newspaper, this was clear proof that those who played this heinous game did get into trouble. The lesson appeared indisputable and the only interesting question was which of the gamblers had grabbed most money when the police pounced.

It was surprising that there was not more gambling and crime in this tough area. Across the entry from us was 'Paddy's Lodge', a dingy lodging house for vagrants, though some men were permanent residents. I often went there to run errands for some of the men, and I always wanted to leave as soon as I could. In a large, badly lit room which smelled of stale cabbage the men sat around quietly with an air of restrained regret. The lodge was governed by a small, spry man named Andy, who maintained strict order. The atmosphere was probably due to Andy's inflexible discipline; though I rarely heard him raise his voice, there was no argument when he spoke. I always felt it should be called 'Andy's Lodge' until someone patiently explained to me in later years that most of the lodgers were Irish. They included some strange characters: a man named Nicholas, who hummed all day and spent most of his time in church; a tall, stooping man we called Uncle Tom, who never stopped talking aloud to himself, but seemed harmless enough. Another, whose identity we never knew, occasionally left cats hanging by their tails and sometimes by their necks. Looking back, it was remarkable that no children were ever molested.

The Roman Catholic Church was influential, and the power of the priest was more important than that of the policeman; when trouble occurred the instinctive reaction was to send someone for the priest. His presence seemed to defuse any explosive situation, though this was due as much to his authoritative attitude as to respect for the cloth. The Church was strong because many Irishmen, Poles and Lithuanians lived in the area. Irish families emigrated during the great potato famine in the middle of the 19th century, and in the late 1880s the Poles and Lithuanians fled from Czarist religious persecutions. They settled in the Wellington Street area, many of them finding work in Bolton's copper works nearby, where I was to become a troublesome strike leader years later. Some of the most common names in our streets were Karalius, Rooskie, Steponevitch, O'Niell, Redmond and Murphy. (One young lad named Vincent Karalius played Rugby League for Great Britain and his younger brother, Frank, married my niece.)

These were also the most common names in St Patrick's Catholic elementary school which was a blackened old building adjoining the church. To reach it, I crossed a patch of waste ground at the end of Wellington Street, half circled a copper smelting factory and walked three hundred yards up the road. Boys and girls were kept separated, but this was the only segregation in the school. All boys from the age of nine to fourteen were taught, in five forms, in one long room; it was divided by curtains and in the middle the headmaster sat in state—a terrifying figure!

He was small but appeared to us ten feet tall when driven to anger. When he bawled, five forms quivered and if he shouted about singing, which he often did, he seemed to regard it as a personal challenge to roar above forty boys in full song. This did not help lessons in other forms very much, particularly as the headmaster had his own boys strategically placed to dominate the room. Forms three and four were at one end of the room, five and six at the other end with the senior form seven placed majestically in the centre.

Led by 'Master' himself, the senior class was the centrepiece of our school lives: on their success or failure our tranquillity depended. No wonder we were apprehensive at the prospect of going into 'standard seven'. Even when the Head was silent it did not necessarily mean all was well. Sometimes it meant he was poised to assault some victim with roars of anger, cuffs on the head or strokes of the cane; to this day I can recall roars of his favourite epithets, 'fool', 'idiot', 'jackass', as he thundered at some unfortunate pupil and his rage reverberated around the room. Yet he was apparently a sentimental man too; few things pleased or soothed him more than to listen to his class singing the Scottish ballads he loved. 'Vair me o, o ro van o—sad am I without thee', we sang uncomprehendingly but anxious to please. Or more briskly, 'Oh, the far Coolins are putting love on me, as step I wi' my cromak to the Isles.'

At the time I never pondered the mystery of why the headmaster of St Patrick's Irish Catholic elementary school made us parrot these Scottish ballads. His wish was our command. Perhaps he felt it his duty to remind us of the other parts of our British heritage, though he never taught us a Welsh song. Or maybe he was displaying a streak of perversity which was perfectly in character.

Our music lessons, which I enjoyed, were conducted by a teacher who was also the choirmaster. He was greatly respected by the boys as a hard, fair, intelligent man who loved music and demanded high standards. Many school hours were spent perfecting the singing of hymns for Mass or Benediction. Some of them were quite beyond our understanding because they were in Latin and we had no knowledge of the language. We were singing in a foreign tongue yet the teacher's love for music communicated itself to us and he fired us with his enthusiasm. He discreetly helped this along by telling us that singing hymns was twice as good for our souls as saying prayers.

We sensed the mood and message of the hymns and sang accordingly. The Good Friday lament was sung with sympathy while the Easter hallelujah was delivered with high-spirited rapture. I had a strong soprano voice and I was delighted to be one of the small choir of four boys who sang verses between the general chorus. It pleased us when we heard that people thought it was one boy singing alone when we sang together. Religion and music were regarded as important and most of the music was religious, apart from 'Master's' irascible attempts to teach us his Scottish ballads.

The school's rugby and swimming feats were a source of great pride to us; it had a particularly good record at swimming and frequently won the town's school shield and the Catholic schools' shield. To us, the Catholic trophy was more desirable and there was jubilation in our streets when the team ran through them in triumph. Being a poor swimmer, I had special admiration for the team as they carried off successive trophies. I was discouraged from swimming because of an ailment which seemed minor at the time—a perforated ear-drum.

I was never outstanding in examinations at school and usually came about tenth out of forty boys. My best subjects were arithmetic—we just about learned decimals and vulgar fractions before leaving—and English, though this never went far beyond the stage of identifying nouns, verbs and adjectives. In subjects I disliked—history and geography—my standard was low, but I was never unduly bothered by this, nor was anyone else. It was good enough to keep me out of trouble with the teachers and that was all I expected.

Some teachers could be rough on boys who, they felt, were not trying and the cane was used frequently, but it was not generally abused. We were always caned on the hand, which could sting quite painfully; the choirmaster in particular was strict but never unfair, and we feared his displeasure. It was possible, with some teachers, to exercise the fine art of withdrawing an outstretched hand at the last split second, as the cane reached the fingers, while wincing with simulated pain, but it never worked with the choirmaster: he simply increased the number of strokes. Other methods of countering the punishment were often discussed and we had our share of schoolboy quacks. Some assured us that rubbing resin on the skin before being caned gave great protection; others claimed that laying a hair on the hand would reduce the force of the stroke.

I never got hold of any resin but I remember my disappointment after unsuccessfully experimenting with the hair a few times.

When we were eleven years old we moved into the form of one teacher who seemed to enjoy using the cane. He was a small, hectoring man who upset one of my best friends by constant caning, though some of it was deserved. Resin and hairs on the hand were useless, so my friend decided to enlist the help of his father, a tall, gangling Irishman with a violent temper. He hit his son much more often than the teacher did, but when he heard the boy's tale of maltreatment and alleged total innocence, that was different.

He lay in wait for the teacher at the corner of Wellington Street, while we watched from a distance. As the teacher reached the corner he was swung round almost off his feet and a long argument ensued. Too far off to hear, we wondered what the effect would be the following day; we went into school together and the teacher, ignoring me, greeted my friend like a long-lost son. I was astonished, as I never dreamed the ploy would be so successful. Later he was made a prefect, almost becoming the teacher's pet; I was a little envious, reflecting that violent protest was well worth while, and I regretted more than ever the absence of a father.

There was an intimate relationship between the school and church and we had regular visits from the priests. Missing a service was worse than muffing a lesson. One enterprising teacher, trying to stimulate enthusiasm by establishing the 'house' system used in public schools, divided the form into four groups and named each of them after a saint—we called them St Pat's, St Mick's, St John's and St Joe's. Points were awarded to each for scholastic and sporting achievements but most points could be earned by going to Mass and Communion. St John's was rarely beaten because some members of its team attended Mass and Communion every morning. I was not a bad churchgoer but I could not compete with that kind of record. Sunday morning Mass was compulsory. To miss it was considered a mortal sin; in addition one had to report it to the teacher on Monday morning.

I sang in the choir at Sunday morning Mass and evening Benediction. Each had its own distinctive atmosphere. The Mass was austere, dutiful and solemn, with the priest's sermon an occasion for a long lecture to the silent congregation. Benediction was a warmer and more relaxed occasion which I enjoyed; there was a musky warmth about it, the sweet smell of incense heavy in the air and clusters of candle lights flickering in the church. It had an aura of sanctity and when the blessing was bestowed it seemed the culmination of an act of genuine piety. On these occasions I sang from the heart.

Although I was pious I was also flippant. The choir occupied a high balcony at the back of the church and every Sunday night a bald-headed man sat directly below me; I used to compete with a mischievous friend to see who could form a bubble on his tongue and then blow it down on the inviting head. Though we became competent marksmen he never complained. Choirboys took it in turn to pump the organ, which meant working up and down a sort of oar at the side. Two of us would pump together, watching an indicator that showed the air level; after an energetic bout of pumping we would sit back and watch the indicator slide down. Each of us waited to see if the other's nerve would break first before one grabbed the handle. If we were late, the organ wheezed discordantly and we were in trouble with the choirmaster.

The choir had to be present at some more solemn ceremonies: before a burial the coffin would lie in the aisles surrounded by candles while mourners knelt nearby. I did not understand the words I sang because they were in Latin and 'De profundis clamavi, ad te Dominum' were beyond my understanding—yet during the sad ceremony I shared the grief. Afterwards it was forgotten as I went out to play football, but in church I was momentarily touched by sorrow and reflected it in my singing.

My sisters Helen and Mary were more devout than I was and attended church frequently. Helen, two years older than I, assumed responsibilities in the home quite early. She had a quieter disposition, patiently accepting the exuberance of Mary and myself while she helped with domestic chores. Mary, four years younger than Helen, was a lively personality although she in turn played her part in running the home. The knowledge of the excessive burden carried by our mother drew us even closer together as we tried to help in any small way we could. Both my sisters were excellent scholars at St Patrick's but they had no chance of furthering their education. Attendance at a Catholic grammar school in a neighbouring town involved costs of uniform, books and travel which my mother could not afford.

As a result, when they left school at the age of fourteen they had to take menial jobs. Helen went into 'service' in a house in Liverpool, cleaning, cooking and doing odd jobs. She was paid only five shillings a week for this and was, of course, unable to save anything. Although she intensely disliked both the work and her isolation from home and friends, she could not leave until her uniform was paid for; at the rate of one shilling a week deducted from her wages, it took five months.

Mary went to work in a nearby bag factory, a prison-like building with small windows that were always closed; they were barred and covered by wire mesh to keep vandals out but looked as if they were designed to keep the girls in. The work entailed long hours for low pay but the only alternative, for those not prepared to stay, was unemployment. This economic pressure, the factories and their conditions, were at once a product and a part of the environment.

My mother remarried and before her second husband, Jim Dooley, died a few years later she had another daughter, Margaret. Although much younger than the three of us, Margaret grew up to share the joys and sorrows of the tiny home and was a greatly loved member of our family. The three girls were as deeply affectionate to our mother as I was but they gave more practical assistance in the home than I did—and they developed an early and lasting tolerance of my foibles.

3

Off to Work

My fourteenth birthday, December 6th, 1936, marked the end of my school education. I did not leave St Patrick's until a few weeks later but boys attending school between their birthday and the end of term were regarded as visitors rather than pupils. The question of going on to the local grammar school never arose because it was non-Catholic; this accounted for the indifference of priests and teachers towards it. Economic pressure reinforced sectarian prejudice and boys went to work as soon as possible to assist their families.

Most boys became labourers in the chemical factories which dominated the town, although a few lucky ones were given office jobs or promised apprenticeships to craftsmen when they were sixteen. Fathers usually spoke for their sons and boys were unlikely to be apprenticed without this informal nepotism. Since there was no one to speak for me, I decided to apply to the giant Imperial Chemical Industries group for an office job; anyone who worked there was envied for his security and reasonably good wages. After waiting in vain for some weeks for a reply to my application, I tried for a job at a large asbestos factory across the town, a branch of the Turner & Newall Company. I was taken on as a labourer, with a terse instruction to present myself at 7.30 on the following Monday morning.

I felt a sense of adventure, tinged with apprehension, as I left 34 Wellington Street at 6.30 one cold January morning to catch the bus to my first job. I carried an old tea can containing tea, sugar and condensed milk, and a packet of bacon sandwiches which had been lovingly prepared and wrapped in old newspaper by my mother. Although she was proud that I was starting work, she was also a little anxious. We were both conscious that this was the beginning of a new era in my life, with new relationships and new responsibilities. I wore long trousers for the first time and a pair of leather clogs with metal reinforcements—like horseshoes—on the wooden soles and heels. With an injunction from my mother to 'be careful' I clattered down Wellington Street in the darkness of

[37]

that winter morning to join queues of workmen at the bus stop.

It was a jolting change in my way of life but I felt no deep sense of unease on the crowded bus. There was an air of purposeful activity and although the atmosphere was earthy it was by no means unfriendly. I was alert and curious. On that novel journey I began to catch the moods of industry which I came to know so intimately in the years ahead: bawdy banter, passionate arguments about football, dogmatic assertions about the job and the bosses, and an underlying sense of comradeship, a feeling that we were all in it together.

At the factory I joined a group of young boys to be shown around a vast shed where asbestos was moulded; we were told that our job was to supply the workmen on the factory benches with tools collected from women at a store. It soon became apparent that new boys were butts for old jokes. One moulding tool was called a baby, and the men had as much fun ordering us to ask for one as the women had in responding to our requests. The ribaldry caused me more embarrassment than it would any fourteen-year-old today. When the men had exhausted their standard repertoire of jokes about babies, busts and bottoms, left-handed spanners, sky hooks and barrow-loads of steam, we were allowed to settle down to the humdrum work of the factory. I adapted to the routine fairly quickly and although I disliked the dirt and noise I was glad to be earning money for the family.

My wages were 12s 3d a week and I felt proud taking them home; they were a supplement to the family income though hardly a passport to luxury. By the time I had deducted bus fares and accepted a little spending money there was not much for the family. Within weeks I felt dissatisfied at the poor pay and sought a better-paid job. My mother, anxious at these early signs of a radical, questing nature, urged me to settle down, but a few weeks later I received an unexpected reply to my application for a job at ICI. After an interview with the Labour Officer I was accepted.

Although my new job was not specified, I went home delighted with the idea of working in an office and no longer in the grime of the factory floor. The assumption was unfounded. I presented myself wearing a collar and tie, only to discover that I was to be a labourer in a long, wide shed full of carboys and tanks of formic acid. The carboys were large bulbous bottles of thick glass, about two feet high and nearly as wide, encased in metal containers lined with straw, which were stacked six-high at the end of the shed

before being filled from one of six large tanks of acid nearby. A
team of boys wheeled them away to be prepared for despatch before
they were loaded on to lorries and railway wagons on either side
of the shed. The work was quite hard and not always safe.

My first job was to hammer the corks tightly into the necks of
the bottles, then tie pieces of sacking over them with a piece of
string. The corks—nearly three inches in diameter—quickly became
saturated with acid, so that when I hit them with a large wooden
mallet they sent up a fine spray. This was unpleasant and uncomfortable, but there were worse hazards. One day, as I tried to hit a badly
fitting cork, I hit the glass and shattered the carboy with a tremendous crash. It was unnerving, but my instinctive reaction caused
some amusement: 'It must have been cracked,' I claimed.

I discovered another way of smashing the glass containers when
I had tried to pack them into metal cases. A protective layer of
straw, on the bottom and all round the casing's interior, was intended to make a tight fit. The bottles were placed inside and had
to be forced down as low as possible, for if they were above the
casing they would be smashed when they were stacked on top of
each other. I would hold the casing with my left hand, grip the
neck of the bottle with my right hand, and lever them high in the
air with my knee before banging them down on the ground. Too
much straw on the bottom made it impossible to force the bottle
in; but the first time I used too little, I shattered the carboy as I
hurled it down. This was even more spectacular than breaking it
with the wooden mallet. My workmates began to warn each other,
with mock solemnity, of the grave danger to life and limb from
flying glass when I was busy.

They looked on these mishaps with a tolerant eye, as well they
might because they were scarred from their own earlier experiences;
but when I progressed to become a 'filler' of the carboys I developed
a foible which upset them. The supply tanks from which the carboys
were filled had to be replenished as they emptied. To do this I had
to open the taps of large pipes connected to the floor above, where
the acid was produced, and as acid gushed into the tanks it was
important to keep checking the level to avoid an overflow. But
carboys were filled at the same time as the supply tanks and I was
neither as concerned nor vigilant as I ought to have been; my tanks
began to overflow with alarming regularity.

The results were unpleasant for everyone because the fumes were

[39]

noxious and even after hosing water and sprinkling sawdust they remained troublesome for hours. My mates were as unconcerned as I was about the loss of acid but in their own interest one of them reported me to the boss and after a severe reprimand I was more careful. It was one of my earliest lessons as a worker in industry that you could damage yourself or your firm if you wished but you could not damage your workmates and get away with it.

For the next two years I worked in that shed. The work was drab and uninteresting, but I was not unhappy; I accepted the job as a necessity and learned how to do the minimum of work without getting into trouble. On one occasion I miscalculated. The foreman told me to sweep the floor of the shed, a job I particularly disliked because it added fine dust to unpleasant fumes. The foreman watched through a window in his office as I ambled the full length of the shed—several hundred yards—brushing slowly as I went; when I got to the end I strolled back to my starting point and began to sweep another strip. Striding from his office the angry foreman reprimanded me for wasting time, and demonstrated how to do the job by sweeping briskly across the width of the shed and back. I had to submit to the rebuke and I swept vigorously for a few moments while he stood and watched, but when he returned to his office my work-rate fell again. I was embarrassed by his angry demonstration before my workmates. Of course he was justified, but I felt aggrieved rather than repentant.

The foreman was a stern man and I regarded him with a mixture of suspicion and hostility, though it was he who had good reason to be suspicious and hostile. No doubt he knew that many of us could work much harder if we tried, for he often caught us playing football in the road outside long after the end of our midday meal break. He turned a blind eye to many of our tricks and even when we practised judo on the straw during working hours he would walk past apparently without noticing. But he could not overlook such unpardonable occasions as when he found one of my workmates giving an acrobatic display, dangling by his legs from a girder high above the straw; he sacked him on the spot. It was proof to us that there was no justice in industry and we nursed our youthful grievance for a long time.

Most of the men were tolerant of the boys—who mixed a generous proportion of play with their work—providing they were not kept waiting for essential supplies of carboys. We had no production line stopping for an official tea-break, but we drank plenty of tea during the day. Each man and boy brought tea, sugar and milk and made a brew in his own tea can at different times. A regular pattern was established so that we knew whose brew was available at a given time. The shout of 'brew up' indicated that each can lid had been filled with hot tea. They were pleasant and frequent breaks and I took my turn in making my own brew and calling my workmates.

I had a very old, chipped tea can which my mother found somewhere and gave to me when I started work. It never occurred to me that this might not be acceptable to my workmates and in any case I could not afford a new one. One day, after one of the boys thanked me for his tea and walked away with it, I happened to follow him round a corner. To my astonishment, I saw him pouring it down a drain. He was embarrassed when I asked him about it, then he admitted that the condition of my old tea can was too much for him and he poured my tea away every day after pretending to sip it. Apparently one of the other boys, with a mischievous imagination, told him what he thought my grandfather did in the tea can. The incident illustrated to me the relative nature of poverty; I felt like a pauper among the poor, but I gave in to this first pressure to keep up with the Joneses and bought a new can.

Two years later, when I was sixteen years old, I decided to leave ICI and try to get a better-paid job elsewhere. This caused consternation at home; the idea of abandoning the security of a job with ICI was practically unthinkable at that time. My stepfather, an unskilled man, was unemployed for long periods; he was incredulous and indignant when I told him I intended to give up my job, but I would not be dissuaded. It was 1939, and as the war was seemingly imminent, more jobs were available.

I took a job delivering coal for a local coal merchant; it was heavy work, filling hundredweight bags of coal, carrying them on my back from a lorry into houses, and emptying them in cramped spaces beneath stairs. I was paid a few shillings more but I certainly earned it. Not only was the work harder, I missed the congenial company and comradeship of the factory. The coal merchant laid down 'heads I win, tails you lose' conditions, so that if I had time off I was not paid for it, but if I worked overtime I received no money for that either. The work was dusty and dirty and I used to go home looking like a miner, but without a miner's pay.

I soon left and wandered from one casual job to another. Most of them were hard, with a large labour turnover, so that it was impossible to make worthwhile friendships, though the pay was a little above average. Finally I got a job at the factory nearest to my home. It was a copper-smelting works, a few hundred yards from Wellington Street, with a reputation for tough bosses and heavy work, but the wages were reasonable—or so I was led to believe. In this sprawling, dirty factory half-a-dozen furnaces smelted up to fifty tons of copper a day. The furnaces were about twenty feet long and ten feet wide and each was loaded through a hatch about three feet square. Slabs of copper weighing three hundredweight, too heavy to be lifted by hand, had to be winched on to the flat end of a fourteen feet long iron paddle which rested on the base of the hatch. It was held at the other end by four burly men who ran and propelled it into the furnace to splay the heavy slabs all around. Four sweating men running in and out of the blinding heat, swinging heavy slabs from their paddles, made a compelling spectacle; their fierce choreography never ceased to fascinate me.

At other times the furnace was loaded with copper scrap which had to be shovelled in. Two hatches were used, one on each side of the furnace, and four men using long-handled spades threw the metal diagonally. It required strength and a sure sense of physical rhythm to throw heavy spadefuls far and accurately. On rare occasions the scrap would go in one side and out the other, provoking a loud and angry reaction from the men on the receiving end, which wasn't only because of the danger involved.

Skill was important, but so was vigour; there was no question of slacking because it created unacceptable tension in the team. Every spadeful was hard work and the heat and exhaustion were so great that when each pair of men had sweated through a spell of ten minutes they were replaced by two others for the same period.

The most common method of discharging the molten metal was literally to hand-ladle it; six men, with no more protective clothing than a pair of gloves, circulated round a hatch cut waist high just above the level of the molten metal and ladled the metal into a row of moulds. Their job was even more difficult than loading the hot furnace. The ladle handles were only as long as the average golf club and the men had to dip them continuously into the searing liquid to unload fifty tons. If moisture was inadvertently left in the moulds after cleaning, the molten metal exploded and cascaded in the air like some fearful fireworks display—

and everyone ducked or ran for cover.

Within minutes of starting work the ladlers were lathered in sweat, but they drank more than sufficient beer to compensate. Just before opening time a boy went to the pub with a basketful of bottles of all shapes and sizes. Despite such a mixed assortment of unlabelled bottles, the boy easily identified them. The furnace—and the bottles —were empty at 1 p.m. when the men went to the pub along the road for more beer. A few of them claimed that they drank fifteen pints a day, and this was probably no exaggeration, but they never seemed wildly drunk.

As soon as the metal solidified, the moulds were kicked over and the red-hot copper, in shapes like artillery shells, was knocked out with a sledgehammer and metal punch held by tongs. Even at that stage there were risks, because the shells had to be loaded six at a time on to a hand truck and pulled out of the refinery. One day the man pulling the truck slipped and fell, and the scorching shells rolled down on the back of his legs.

Life in the factory was tough but I enjoyed the company of the boys who were my workmates. I was now a high-spirited sixteen-year-old, slim but strong. Years of hard work were developing my body and some practice in judo and boxing had begun to give me self-confidence in the rough no-nonsense atmosphere of the gang. I quickly settled down and made some great friends. Although our job of wheeling copper bars to the furnace on long-handled trucks was hard work, we never made heavy weather of it. Naturally exuberant, we often raced each other with the trucks, though we were careful to return more slowly so that no more bars were wheeled than was expected. We chattered all the time as we dragged the trucks up and down the factory—discussing girls, rugby foot-ball, the bosses, the local gossip.

Before knocking off work at 5 p.m. we dispersed into the most unlikely parts of the factory. It was generally accepted that the first boy to get a good truck or wheelbarrow at 7.30 a.m. could have it for the rest of the day; rickety ones were harder to pull. So when work was finished we hid our prized trucks in dark sheds, under old sacking, behind railway wagons, and even inside unlit furnaces. We were supposed to begin work immediately after clocking on in the morning but we invariably spent some time recovering trucks or searching for better ones before slowly getting down to the job of providing tons of copper for the furnaces.

Lunchtime, which we called dinner time, was from twelve noon till one o'clock and some of us often went home because we lived so near the factory. Usually, after a quick meal, I went back at 12.30 to enjoy the company and whatever fun was available. One of our favourite tricks was to creep to a three-wheeler vehicle which stood outside the garage where the foreman had his lunch. We would release the brake quietly and gently push it a few hundred yards away. Out of earshot we would start the engine and career around the factory at hair-raising speeds. We were always careful to return the vehicle, with the engine switched off, just before 1 o'clock when the foreman would emerge, apparently unaware of our escapades. But he must have heard of them. Although we were never caught red-handed, our joy rides were suddenly ended by an order that vehicles should be locked inside the garage during dinner time. We then had to rely on football, wrestling and cards to occupy our dinner hours.

Despite the fun the job was demanding, and apart from our un-official tea breaks there was little respite from feeding the furnaces. I took a strong dislike to the foreman's attitude and often clashed sharply with him; he was a curt, sharp-spoken man who always wore a black suit and looked like a bereaved undertaker. His word was law and I marvelled at the submissiveness of the men as he issued instructions. Every morning at 7.30, as the factory hooter sounded, the foreman approached the waiting men who had to stand near one of the furnaces. Pointing to each man in turn he barked out his orders: 'Load No. 22 furnace.' 'Load No. 24.' 'Unload two wagons of coal', and to the boys: 'Get the bars down to No. 22', or 'No. 24' or whatever the furnace happened to be. After allocating jobs to everyone present he stood with his back to the furnaces awaiting latecomers. I was usually among them and when I arrived, often breathless, he would give me a job coupled with the threat 'I'm not standing for this'.

I always thought the men looked like cattle as they waited to be allocated jobs; but apparently this method was an improvement on the one used in the days of mass unemployment. Then the men waited outside the gate, hoping for a day's casual work, and the manager would point to the strongest, who were duly grateful for the favour. Although I understood the history, I was puzzled that the men should still allow themselves to be treated in this way— especially as it was 1939 and, with the country preparing for war

[44]

unemployment had been reduced.

I did not closely follow the political events of the Munich period but it was clear by mid-1939 that war was inevitable. This confirmed the unlikely comment made some years earlier by the Irish father of my closest friend. Emotionally and confusingly he reiterated his conviction that war was 'sure to come when Itly and Muscolina get together'. I could not puzzle this out, because I vaguely understood that Italy was under the dictatorial rule of Mussolini anyhow—but we never dreamed of challenging my friend's father. Much later the riddle was resolved when I discovered that by 'Itly' he meant Hitler, and despite his flamboyant mispronunciation his prophecy was not far out.

Like everyone else we did not know how war would affect our lives. The men of Wellington Street and the surrounding area had suffered grievously in the set-piece battles of the First World War and we were brought up on bloodcurdling tales of Passchendaele and the Somme. I was nearly seventeen when the Second World War broke out and I looked forward to fighting in the air force if it lasted till I was eighteen.

In the meantime I was given a man's job at the factory. I was quick to demand a man's wages, although excuses were advanced why I should not get it—'not just yet'. But like my friends I was less concerned with the work than I was with joining the armed forces: shortly after my eighteenth birthday I was called up and applied to be an air gunner in the Royal Air Force. I did not know what the educational requirements were, but mine soon proved inadequate. I was sent to a camp at Padgate, near Warrington, for three days of intensive tests, but I was dismissed after the first day. Obviously I fell well below the desired standard. Bitterly disappointed at this rejection, I joined the Army shortly afterwards and served in the Royal Army Service Corps.

After less than a year I was discharged on health grounds. The slight difficulty with my hearing had not seriously disturbed me while I was working in the factories, but during my army service my hearing deteriorated and after a series of medical boards I was discharged. When I returned to Wellington Street I discussed the problem with my own doctor, who arranged for me to see an ear, nose and throat specialist at the ancient Widnes Accident Hospital. One of my eardrums had a serious perforation as the result of the early infection and the consultant was able to patch it up. I did not understand the rest of his treatment but he improved my hearing. I was able to go back to work without fear of the increasing burden of deafness which had seemed probable during my spell in the Army.

4

Shop Steward

When I returned from the Army to work at Bolton's copper factory I was given the heavy job of loading furnaces. Little had changed; work and discipline were still hard, but plenty of overtime was available, though the foreman refused it to anyone who displeased him. Everybody wanted the extra pay for weekend work but if they stepped out of line they did not get it; overtime, and some of the less exacting labouring jobs, were given to the most docile as carrots for conformity.

It was remarkable that a factory with domineering management, old-fashioned processes and poor working conditions had no powerful trade union organisation. Although the craftsmen belonged to their craft unions, only four out of about four hundred workers were members of a general union for the unskilled. There seemed to be no general desire for organisation and the employers dictated terms with little or no opposition. Bad industrial relations went hand-in-hand with old industrial methods. Men who loaded furnaces manually had neither modern equipment nor effective machinery for collective bargaining. This would have been surprising if there had been no history of local trade union activity, but the first unions were established in Widnes in the 1890s and they were quite strong before the First World War. A basis for effective organisation may have been laid in other factories, but no worthwhile legacy was left at Bolton's.

Although I was always prepared to argue with authority, especially in the factory, I too never gave any serious thought to trade unionism. But my attitude changed after I had an emergency operation for appendicitis, followed by a few weeks' convalescence. I returned to the factory and explained that I was unable to load furnaces until I had fully recovered; needing money, I asked for a temporary light job—such as sweeping the factory floor—which was sometimes given to men who had been ill. The foreman refused; he said I could start work again when I was able to load the furnaces and not before.

That day I decided that the factory needed trade union organisation and I would do the organising if necessary. During the afternoon a friend told me that the Chemical Workers Union had many members in other factories. Within 24 hours I met the secretary of the Widnes branch to discuss the best means of organising Bolton's, and although the connection between copper smelting and the chemical industry was not obvious to me I accepted his assurance that we were eligible to join his union. When I eventually returned to the factory I was fit, broke, angry and bitter—and supplied with hundreds of application forms.

The response of my workmates when I asked them to join was encouraging; they were willing to enlist and eager to take action against an employer who had never been seriously challenged. The men were ready to make such a challenge but it had to be planned, organised and unexpected. Moving surreptitiously from one department to another, I contacted those men who would be most likely to influence their workmates. The management began to suspect my activities but this was a spur rather than a deterrent because the sooner we had a strong organisation the less likely I was to be picked off. A general staff was the first requirement and I carefully selected the strongest and most articulate characters to be shop stewards in each department. Some of them became over-enthusiastic about recruiting new members but I was anxious that no strong-arm tactics should be used. Apart from this, each steward was encouraged to develop his own individual approach to workers who refused to join. Most tried persuasion and force of argument; a few used ridicule or contempt.

It is difficult to differentiate between a worker who objects to joining a union on conscientious grounds and another who is prepared to undermine the organisation if doing so will ingratiate him with the employers while he takes advantage of benefits won by the union. The shop stewards respected genuine objectors but they had little time for the bosses' men. Except for this small unenthusiastic minority nearly all the men were eager to join and within three weeks we had organised over four hundred workers, which was almost all those eligible. The organisation began to take shape and develop its character.

I had been contacting the shop stewards individually until the time came for our first meeting in the factory. It had to be secret because we were not recognised by a hostile management. One of the shop stewards, a crane driver, arranged for us to meet in the

garage, and as the men slipped in one by one I took stock. They
were a tough bunch. If they could be welded into a team the
management was in for a shock. I asked each of them in turn to
report on the membership and organisation in his own department.
Sid Hillier, a lantern-jawed Hercules who rarely spoke, was responsible for transport. He simply said: 'All in, no problems.'
Jim Ratcliffe, representing the ladlers, was still in his sweat shirt
and thick trousers. All his men had joined without question. Tom
Cosgrove, a burly, barrel-chested furnace loader, said: 'Most are
in—the rest will soon follow.'

So it went on, showing that in every department we had formidable strength. It remained to elect a leader as spokesman and to
formulate demands. I was only twenty years old with no experience
of trade union organisation, but I was unanimously elected chairman
of the committee. We decided that our first demand should be for
recognition and negotiating rights.

Later that day I went to see the Labour Relations Officer. Although more of a diplomat than the rest of the management he
had to express their policy. He explained that they were unable to
recognise the union since they already had an agreement with another
one. My argument that the other union had less than half a dozen
members left him quite unmoved. The firm's factory in Stafford-
shire employed many members of the other union and the management took this into account in deciding their attitude. I was angry
but not surprised. His ploy was to express regret that I should be
disappointed, but he said he knew I would appreciate that he must
accept management's decision. I knew that fulminating would not
affect him; power lay elsewhere. But remembering those tough
figures in the garage I countered with a ploy of my own. I suggested
he should tell the management that they were now dealing with a
powerful and unpredictable group—and said I knew he would
appreciate that I must accept their decision.

The management's refusal to recognise us was a severe—and
potentially lethal—blow to our organisation. It angered the men
at first but I knew that if we failed to win recognition and were
unable to represent them they would eventually lose heart. I raised
the matter immediately in the Widnes branch of the union to which
I had now become an accredited delegate. Naturally its members
supported our claim and the North-West Area Organiser, Bob
Edwards (now Labour MP for Bilston), who was a full-time official,

made representations on our behalf. We decided to make no move until his discussions were concluded, hoping that he would succeed, but the management were firm and unbending. Many of the men demanded a strike but I was by no means eager for one. I was deeply uneasy about strikes while the war was on, especially after serving in the Army. I wanted negotiating rights without a strike, but the employers' continued hostility convinced us that they were exploiting the situation as an excuse for rejecting our union and depressing wages. At a meeting to consider action, I suggested that if we threatened a strike the management would reconsider and meet our demands. But the men were in an angry mood and they voted almost unanimously for a strike although they also accepted my proposal that we should give twenty-one days' notice.

Although we were taking unofficial action, we had the tacit support of the union, and its officials encouraged us. For the first time the management's attitude began to soften a little, but they still refused to negotiate, insisting that the committee should recommend calling off the threatened strike. We refused, so just before the notice expired they decided to speak to the men directly. A mass meeting was called near one of the furnaces and after I had addressed it the Manager took over.

He completely misunderstood the mood of the men, seeming to assume that they were being misled by irresponsible and destructive militants. Before he got very far with his lecture someone switched on the large fan used for cooling men and molten metal. This was a noisy machine and when other workers began scraping their spades on the stone floor he gave up and walked out. The men were jubilant at the success of their unprecedented display of defiance. When I addressed them again they voted to confirm the decision to strike. I suggested we should all meet the following day—outside the gates—and the meeting broke up. Workers put their tools away, damped down the furnaces, and headed for home. Next day in an atmosphere of near disbelief the men found themselves outside the gates for their first dispute. A strike in Widnes was a rare event—a strike at Bolton's was unheard of. Brinkmanship had failed to move the employers, but it had certainly moved the men.

The management still refused technical recognition to the union but agreed to negotiate with us at any time. On this uneasy compromise the strike committee decided to recommend a return to work, although I knew that the men would probably expect more from us than we could get from the management across an unofficial negotiating table. That night we held a meeting of the Widnes branch of the union in a public house near the factory. While we were discussing the strike committee's recommendation, tempers flared. One of the burly shop stewards, defending the decision, was attacked by the angry Irishman from Wellington Street who later committed suicide with his own razor. My main achievement at the meeting was not in persuading the branch to accept our recommendation but in keeping these two apart. At the next day's mass meeting I called for a resumption of work and, although this was hardly popular, the men eventually agreed.

My life in the factory was now transformed and every kind of grievance was brought to me by groups and individuals; each day I discussed them with the Labour Relations Officer and foremen in various departments. My own foreman was disdainful and determined to ignore the union. Before long I knew who would receive me with cold hostility and who would be responsive to representations. Although the Labour Relations Officer proved to be much more tolerant than I had expected, the senior management remained dogmatic and inflexible.

Our members were not all angels—but neither were the bosses. I worked occasionally with a cross-eyed labourer who used one swear word to every two other words. He had served time in jail and sometimes boasted to me about how easy it was to steal from the works' stores. 'But it's easier still for the bosses and they're worse,' he said. One day he proved it. He had stolen some wood from the stores and said that while he was hiding inside, before stealing, he saw a watchman creep in and steal some tins of paint. At 5 p.m. as we walked to the gate to clock off, he made no attempt to conceal the wood. When he was challenged by the watchman he replied: 'It's only wood, not bloody paint', and after a few face-saving comments by the watchman he was allowed to walk out—tough, arrogant, and, in his own view, vindicated.

Union activities were affecting my work as a furnace loader, which was unfair on my workmates as we were on piecework. Through the influence of one of the shop stewards who was a dominant figure in the garage, I became a crane driver, which gave me greater freedom of movement throughout the factory and more opportunity for making contacts. Work became easier for me and at first I wondered if it was a subtle managerial sop. But they were not subtle employers and they remained rigidly opposed to the union. Still denied recognition, the shop stewards' committee continued to meet in the secrecy of the garage. We were inexperienced but enthusiastic, and soon merged into a strong committee which won the confidence of the men.

Informal procedures for negotiating with the employers were quickly developed and we tackled the difficult job of redressing long-standing grievances. The management agreed to set up a works council which was really a device for informal union recognition because all our shop stewards sat on it. Meetings were useful for discussing working conditions, but the employers insisted that questions of pay should be excluded. Of course this was fundamental and we constantly demanded full negotiations. The issue was to be raised dramatically a few months later when Pay-As-You-Earn Income Tax was introduced.

The management were already keeping a week's pay in hand when suddenly they announced their intention to keep a further two days' pay to give them more time to assess the tax. Their decision was made without consultation and the response to this insensitivity was immediate. The men, already simmering with anger at management's attitude to their union, demanded a strike, but this time we played it differently. Instead of giving twenty-one days' notice, we decided to seek negotiations and, if they failed, stage a lightning strike. A short, sharp lesson would shake the employers out of their complacency. The effects of such a strike on a factory which had molten metal bubbling in the furnaces could be disastrous, but we assumed that the management knew these facts as well as we did.

I told the Labour Officer that the committee intended to meet the Manager next day to discuss the new pay arrangements and, while we were at it, pay for annual leave. When he said that he didn't know whether the Manager would accept the request I told him that it was not a request but an ultimatum. Left in no doubt of our intentions, he promised to pass on the message but, of course, with a marked lack of enthusiasm. I returned to the committee and together we arranged for each shop steward to prepare his men for strike action if necessary.

Each department was run by a manager and foremen. We saw the General Manager only on rare occasions when he made a quick visit to a particular furnace or process. A tall, angular man with a long, sharp nose and an authoritative manner, he was never seen without a stiff, brown trilby hat, even in summer; in winter he also wore a short macintosh. At any rate it always looked short on him but perhaps he could not get one long enough to fit him. He always walked quickly, with a sense of urgency, as if he had just heard of some disaster. Yet he would stop suddenly and dramatically if he spotted workers idling. No words were needed; the icy gaze was sufficient to send them scurrying. I always made it a point of principle, if I was caught idling or drinking tea, to get up and walk very slowly to my job. The movement was a surrender to his authority but it was offered as grudgingly as possible.

The Manager spent most of his time in his office, in a large, dark block, about twenty yards away from the furnaces. This short distance separated two worlds. The office staff men wore clean suits, collars and ties, and the girls neat dresses, whereas we all wore dirty overalls. They came in at nine o'clock in the morning while we clocked in at seven-thirty. They were paid if they were off ill; we were not. Management operated from this block of offices and it was to this citadel that we shop stewards went to put our demands: we headed for the Manager's office at the top of the stairs.

The office staff seemed taken aback as twelve tough working men in overalls and heavy boots appeared among them. No one spoke to the uninvited guests as we entered, but near the top of the stairs the Manager's secretary appeared and said he would not see us. A prim, well-groomed blonde with a chocolate-box type of beauty, she tried to tell us about the evils of strikes and breaking contracts, but we were not interested. We had assumed the Manager was in his office, but as the girl was speaking he suddenly appeared behind us on the stairs, still wearing his trilby, and pushed past us, pausing only to tell a shop steward at the rear of the delegation that as he had no right to be there he was sacked. Then he vanished into the remote confines of his office, leaving us on the stairs. He had taken us by surprise and we all felt out of place on his ground. None of us knew why he should discriminate so oddly against one man, who was a long-serving craftsman. I wondered whether to charge in after him; the flushed girl and the closed door were ahead of me and the shop stewards' committee lined up on the stairs behind me. They all hesitated and I knew it was up to me to make a move.

Conscious of the men's embarrassment and the critical eyes of the office workers, I suggested that we should call the strike immediately and make the reinstatement of the sacked man another condition of our return to work.

There was a chorus of approval and we marched back to the factory where each shop steward went to his own department to give the pre-arranged signals. The effect was startling; few factories can ever have been paralysed so quickly. Within two minutes every man had stopped work while the factory processes ground themselves to a halt. The railway engine, hauling wagons through the factory, stopped dead in its tracks and the driver stepped down. Men who were ladling molten metal from the furnaces left it bubbling: a few who had already filled their ladles took the trouble to walk back and pour the molten metal back into the furnace; for good measure one of them threw the ladle in as well. On another furnace, with a different system of discharge, molten metal was gushing out and filling a series of rapidly moving trucks. Within seconds the trucks stopped moving and tons of molten metal overflowed on to the floor.

The men were jubilant. It had taken only a few minutes to produce chaos, and undoubtedly the factory would soon resemble a disaster area. For the first time the management's nerve broke; the departmental manager came running, urging me to ask the men to clear the molten metal before it solidified on the floor and in the neglected furnace. I was assured that the management would 'do something' about our claim. As I wanted to avoid permanent damage and an urgent decision had to be taken, I agreed. Later that day, after endorsing my decision, the shop stewards' committee decided to recommend a full resumption of work when the management reaffirmed their assurance. This was the result I had hoped for—a short, sudden strike which would shake the employers' complacency. But when I put the strike committee's recommendations to a mass meeting, strong objections were raised. Some men who had been docile for years were now aggressive and wanted a specific promise of money before returning to work. But eventually the majority voted for the proposal. They accepted the argument that if the employers double-crossed us we would stay out next time.

Shortly afterwards we were given our two days' pay and the dismissed craftsman was reinstated. The union became highly popular—as well as increasingly influential. With more cooperation from the management we achieved greater success in what were still called unofficial negotiations; but relationships were more difficult to change. Foremen on the shop floor, whose power had never previously been challenged, were particularly bitter and my own foreman rigidly maintained his cold, contemptuous attitude towards me personally.

One man, a commissionaire, who was violently anti-trade union, took every opportunity to express his feelings. He had the additional job of selling tickets for the factory meals—a week's ticket cost 3s 6d and I occasionally bought them. He developed a nasty habit of becoming engrossed in his work whenever I appeared, leaving me to stand waiting a long time for my ticket. One day, when he had played his usual trick, I paid with a handful of coppers which I said were 84 halfpennies. He refused to accept them but I insisted that he must as they were British currency. Reluctantly he counted the coins and said there were only 83; I maintained there were 84. There was a silent and angry recount until, just before he reached the 83rd, I tossed the additional halfpenny casually on to his desk and warned him that I too could play games. This behaviour was not calculated to endear me to him, but it served its purpose and on the basis of this petty retaliation we achieved a chilly truce.

Within six months of joining the union I became one of the main spokesmen of the Widnes branch and represented it at various conferences. At one large regional conference attended by delegates from all other unions I tried to criticise the union which was impeding our recognition at Bolton's. The chairman ruled me out of order on some technicality but I persisted, and after a barrage of encouragement from the delegates I was allowed to speak. The union I criticised was the National Union of General and Municipal Workers, of which I am now a sponsored member, and the chairman was Ellis Smith, then Member of Parliament for Stoke-on-Trent, South, whose seat I was to inherit many years later.

I was delighted to be appointed a delegate to the union's annual conference in London. I had never been to London, far less to a national conference. Before I went I studied the agenda eagerly; it was a little daunting, with its resolutions on important national issues, but I was not too concerned. At that time—twenty-one years old—I was willing to try my hand at anything. In the Blue Room of the Bonnington Hotel in Bloomsbury, where the conference was held, the leading officials sat at the main table, and the delegates from all over the country at branching tables. The atmosphere exhilarated me and before long I was on my feet speaking against one of the resolutions. When I finished, the conference applauded and I knew as I sat down that I could hold an unfamiliar audience. During the week I spoke in a number of debates and although I was often on the losing side I invariably had a good reception. It was heady stuff for a young man and I enjoyed it.

The dominant figure was the General Secretary, Arthur Gilliam, a white-haired Cockney who, as a speaker, combined an urbane manner with explosive matter. He had a habit of stating, with apparent affability, that he would deal with a recalcitrant firm by taking the factory to pieces 'brick by brick'. This was always well received by the delegates who welcomed his militancy.

I did not know that in the preceding months the reports of my activities in Widnes had been noticed by a very attractive girl who was Arthur Gilliam's secretary. We met at one of the social functions of the conference and developed a mutual affection rather like a shipboard romance. We were both sorry when the conference ended and when we parted she said that 'fate' would decide whether we met again, while I felt it would be 'circumstances'. In the ensuing elections for the National Executive Council I just missed being elected, despite my brief membership of the union. Shortly afterwards I received a letter from the General Secretary saying that a member had suddenly retired and as I had more votes than any of the other candidates, according to the rules I was now on the Executive Council. This meant regular meetings at the London office. Inside the envelope was a personal note on which was written the single word 'Fate'. With my formal reply to the General Secretary I enclosed the note with the word 'Circumstances' written on the reverse side. The day my letter arrived was one of the rare occasions when Arthur Gilliam opened some of his mail himself while his secretary was busy. He must have thought he had an odd new member on his Executive Council, although he never commented on it to me.

Bob Edwards, the North West organiser, had growing power in the union: a rousing orator, he was favourite for the leadership when Gilliam retired. The comradeship displayed by both of them at that conference soon evaporated when Gilliam's leadership was challenged by some members. A special conference was convened to consider charges of malpractices which were made against him

but his supporters fought strongly, trying some ingenious ma-
noeuvres.

The day before the conference I received a telegram informing
me that it was cancelled, but a quick check with Edwards proved
the message false and enabled him to advise all delegates to ignore
similar messages. Although Edwards had my warm support I was
saddened when I arrived at the door of the conference hall to see
Gilliam, the former rumbustious leader, sitting outside, forbidden
to enter. Most people passed him silently but I stopped to have a
word with him. He knew I was one of his most vigorous opponents
yet in those few moments I think we established a personal rapport.

The chairman was a Gilliam supporter and when the conference
was finally convened he played his last card by announcing with
regret that it was out of order, the proceedings invalid and the
meeting was closed—all in the space of three minutes. Of course,
we had anticipated this and an immediate nomination was proposed
from the floor for an alternative chairman who conducted the rest
of the business. Many charges were made during the rancorous
dispute which ended with Edwards being elected General Secretary.
The trouble was not of his choosing and he handled a difficult
situation admirably. But such clashes were bound to weaken the
enthusiasm of shop-floor workers, leaving a sense of bewilderment.
Internal strife of this kind is always debilitating and our union was
weakened by it, although once the struggle was joined it had to be
fought through to the end.

The members at Bolton's were relieved when the trouble was
over. We had been advocating unity on the shop floor and the lack
of it at headquarters was not helpful. But we had enough problems
in the factory without worrying too much about disputes elsewhere.
The management had mellowed since our successful strike, but
they were still sufficiently difficult and obstinate to keep us fully
occupied with our attempts to improve the wages and conditions
of our members.

5

Town Councillor

Although my trade union activities were absorbing and time-consuming, I was not too preoccupied to complain to the landlord about the condition of our house. In one bedroom the rain came directly through holes in the roof and when it fell heavily it would splash over the side of a shallow bowl, so that we had to use a bucket to catch the water. One hole in the gable end was large enough for children to put their arms in and steal anything within reach. No tenant could be content with these conditions—but our landlord was. Prosperous and pompous, he owned other houses around as well as two confectionery and tobacconists' shops nearby; claiming a monopoly of economic wisdom, he rejected my repeated requests for repairs because they would be 'uneconomic'.

Argument was unavailing so I asked the Town Clerk about our legal rights and the Council's responsibility. He referred me to the Rent Act which provided for a forty per cent net rent deduction for houses in a state of disrepair. I sent in an application form and the Public Health authorities came to inspect the house and report to the Town Council. After the inspection, which must have been a derisive formality, 34 Wellington Street was certified unfit and our net rent was reduced by forty per cent. It was the opening shot of a long campaign.

Naturally the landlord was angry and he vented his feelings on my mother shortly afterwards. When I saw how much he had upset her I paid him a courtesy call. In his shop I gave him a free sample of the most vigorous factory invective but, as I could not dent his pride, I decided to damage his pocket; I got hundreds of application forms for rent reductions and delivered them to every house in and around Wellington Street. At first people were a little sceptical, which was not surprising because tenants expected to pay regularly and promptly or be threatened with eviction. Many were surprised at my assurance that they could have their rent reduced so easily.

Visiting the homes of these people moved me deeply. For the first time I realised the extent of the misery and suffering caused by wretched slums which I had taken for granted throughout my childhood. Hundreds of nearby houses needed repairs and many had leaking roofs. One woman showed me how, no matter where she placed her bed, the water would drip on it. In one case, part of the roof had collapsed on a woman who was confined to bed expecting a baby. The roofs and walls of most houses suffered badly from damp which not only affected bedrooms but living rooms and parlours as well. One parlour had eight or nine holes in the bare floor boards, some of them so big that I could put my foot through to the damp earth beneath. The occupant of the house, an old lady, never used the parlour, and once a nasty smell was traced to a dead cat under the floor boards.

In some cases it was possible to crawl from one house to another because of large holes in the walls, caused by damp and the impact of coal tipped against the walls. Coalmen would walk through the kitchen and tip coal under the stairs against the parlour wall. One man said, 'I don't mind the hole so much but old Jones next door comes in at night and pinches my coal.'

A woman complained, 'I've lived in this house for forty years and never had one repair done.' Under the door, where the floor had sunk, she had stuffed sacking into a four-inch gap to keep the draught from her husband who lay dying in the icy room. He was too ill to be moved to hospital and the bedrooms had been unusable for five years. The old lady was chosen as a member of a deputation to complain to the local authorities the following week, but she did not turn up: she was attending the funeral of her husband.

My new insight into an old problem changed my attitude: instead of merely trying to damage the landlord I sought constructive help for the neighbours. Even simple amenities such as dustbins were lacking and dumped rubbish added to the squalor. I urged people to complain to their landlords or the local authority, but it was remarkably difficult to persuade them to act. Poverty stultifies activity, especially among those who have endured it all their lives; it creates a tradition of passivity. Poor people, with lined faces, seldom dreamed of challenging the landlord or officials behind desks at the Town Hall. The poor were expected to keep their place and nearly always did so. If the thought of defying better-off people occurred to them it was rarely acted upon.

I was determined to change conditions and wanted early action. My first request was a straightforward one asking the local authorities to provide people with dustbins. When officials at the Town Hall insisted none were available I decided to hitch-hike to London and find some. Before long I came across an ironmonger's shop with dustbins on display. When I explained the purpose of my visit to the manager he invited me to lunch to discuss it. Understanding what I was trying to do, he promised to reserve a gross of dustbins until he heard from the Town Council; but he warned me to expect problems when I notified the Town Council of our agreement.

After making the arrangement I called on a Widnes-born journalist living in London, Jack Carney. Although writing for an overseas paper, he maintained an interest in his home town and contributed articles to the local newspaper. He asked me for details of the order I had given and the name and address of the manager of the shop and I agreed to keep him informed of developments. Back in Widnes, the Town Clerk received my report with interest and wry amusement. He promised to tell the appropriate committee and convey their decision to the shop in London. Although this was done, the Town Clerk told me afterwards that the offer had been rejected because the cost was 'prohibitive'. It was a disappointing end to my search for dustbins which the Council obviously hoped would soon be forgotten.

Jack Carney had other ideas. He wrote about it in the local newspaper, applauding my 'idealistic' efforts and describing me as 'the knight errant of the dustbins'. His article drew public attention to my activities and many people in the area began to discuss their problems with me. One day the local parish priest visited my home to tell me that he was calling a meeting of tenants to ventilate their grievances; if I would be the main speaker he would act as chairman. I readily agreed. A large and enthusiastic crowd listened to the chairman's opening remarks and then to my own vigorous speech demanding action from the landlords and Council. The local newspaper's report of the meeting quoted the priest's words extensively, and briefly mentioned at the end that I had also spoken. This surprised me but it underlined the difficulties of conveying my views to a wider audience in the town.

Labour Councillors for the Ward were understandably cool towards me since my campaign was an implied rebuke to them. I felt that they were complacent and they probably thought I was intrusive. Instead of placating them I reacted against them and looked elsewhere for support. At that time Bob Edwards was the national chairman of the Independent Labour Party and I began to take a greater interest in the political activities of the ILP. I had only a vague idea of the historical divisions which had racked the ILP and the Labour Party, and naturally the ILP officials I spoke to justified their own Party's stand. The situation in early 1944 seemed clear enough to me after reading ILP literature and talking to some of the Party's regional organisers.

They told me that the ILP was small, militant and dedicated to the purest ideals of socialism; it was unsullied by power and behaved with responsibility. It regarded the Labour Party, more in sorrow than in anger, as well meaning but misguided in its acceptance of an electoral truce during the war. The struggle against Tories, capitalists, speculators and landlords had to be carried on at all times. It sounded fine to me and I joined. There was no branch in Widnes so I helped to organise one and became secretary. We held periodic meetings which were badly attended and I sold copies of the *New Leader*, the Party's newspaper, but the membership never increased. We carried on until the General Election of July 1945.

The European war had ended in May but its shadow remained; shortages, rationing and controls were part of normal life. The major political question was which Party would manage the difficult transition from war to peace and build a fair and prosperous society. It was the first election in nearly ten years and as the Widnes branch of the ILP did not want to split the Labour vote we supported Christopher Shawcross, the Labour candidate. I felt disappointed when I was not asked to speak in support of him but I was invited to appeal for funds at one of his meetings. This small gesture of goodwill neatly avoided any risk of ILP policies being advocated —and underlined the local Labour Party's lurking suspicions.

Polling day was July 5th but because of the large number of postal votes from the armed forces the results were not declared until July 26th. I was working in Bolton's at the time and we were all jubilant at the Labour landslide. The latest figures, chalked in large letters near one of the furnaces, were continually changed as more sweeping gains were broadcast.

Despite the national success my personal relations with local Labour Councillors in my Ward had not improved. Fighting national issues in a general election was exciting, but once it was over we were back to the perennial problems of slum housing. No one else seemed interested, but I was still impatient for action. The Widnes branch of the ILP was fine in theory but weak in practice so I left it soon afterwards and continued my campaign alone.

The municipal elections were due in November and I was asked by neighbours to stand for the Town Council. There were two vacancies in my Ward and two Labour and two Conservative candidates were nominated. Although the Church played no formal part, it supported the Labour candidates, who were both devout Catholics. I decided to fight all of them, standing as a local man without any political label or philosophy, wanting only to improve, or preferably remove, the slums.

My organisation, consisting of a dozen friends, had its campaign headquarters at 34 Wellington Street. Despite a gift of £5 we were desperately short of money, so we raffled packets of cigarettes in the factory to help to pay for the printing of an election address and some posters. As we had no surplus to hire equipment I campaigned without a car or loudspeaker—unlike the other candidates. The only way I could address people was to stand on the street corner and speak up. At my first meeting, near my home in Wellington Street, the only people present were my campaign committee—all twelve of them. They appeared self-conscious before I began but when I addressed them as my audience they became positively embarrassed. Gradually people came out of their houses to listen, but as they did not crowd around there was no sense of occasion. I felt as if I was pricking a deflated balloon.

The atmosphere changed when some of the other candidates appeared. They drowned my voice with their loudspeaker and their chairman, who chatted up a gathering crowd, introduced them as great local statesmen. I could not compete with the loudspeaker but I took advantage of the crowd they attracted. As soon as the chairman ended the meeting with a hearty 'Thank you' I began a tirade against the Town Council and the landlords. This time I won a clear and favourable reaction.

From then on whenever I saw the other candidates with their loudspeakers I repeated the process. They were nonplussed. If they moved off when I appeared at their meetings it looked as if they were running away, and I said so. If they kept talking, I waited until they had finished then criticised their verbosity. It worked so successfully that my supporters would come running to tell me where the other candidates' loudspeakers were operating.

Gradually I began to win strong support in the Ward. Crowds of gay children paraded, chanting and singing and making as much noise as they could with tin cans or anything else that would add to the din. One of my opponents was named Traynor and he was not pleased with the children's chorus:

> Vote vote vote for Jack Ashley
> He's as steady as a rock.
> We'll put him in a ring and crown him as our king
> And we'll throw old Traynor in the dock dock dock.

It was chanted in every street and, with appropriate variations on the name, whenever any of my opponents appeared. Once again they were at a loss for a suitable reaction. Some of them listened meekly and seemed to be defeatist; others tried to drown the children's voices with loudspeakers and appeared to be bullies.

They retaliated with chalked slogans. But no sooner were they written on walls or roads than the children obliterated them and replaced them with mine. When my opponents escalated from chalk to whitewash the children went further and used white paint. It was indelible for a long time and years after the election the slogans were visible.

I canvassed every house in the Ward and the response from people was encouraging. Inevitably I met the tenants who had attended my meetings or whom I had helped directly during the housing campaign; they needed no persuasion. Many people were confident that I would win but as a newcomer to politics I was unable to assess the outcome. All my opponents seemed confident so when the polls closed I walked with my supporters to the count, trying to appear as politically sophisticated as the old hands who were defending their seats. The ballot boxes were opened in a large hall in the town centre, crowded with civic dignitaries, councillors, candidates and their supporters. My contest became a centre of attraction as the votes were counted. To the delight of my friends I topped the poll.

I shared the excitement, and the prospect of espousing my cause on the Town Council pleased me. Some people had opposed my campaign, or had been indifferent, because they felt I was too young to know what I was talking about. Now, at the age of twenty-two, I had become one of the country's youngest councillors and I was eager for action. Local status did not matter much to me but I was exhilarated by the prospect of campaigning on the Council.

In the Town Hall square a large crowd, including a generous quota from my Ward, gave me a warm reception when the result was announced. We celebrated at 34 Wellington Street that night at a party which ended with one of our more exuberant supporters having to be carried home at about 7 a.m. At 7.35 a.m. I was walking to the factory, a little late as usual, treading over slogans of 'Vote for Ashley' chalked on the roads and self-consciously glancing at them on the factory walls.

I was rarely tired at that stage of my life. Neither loss of sleep nor my additional work for the trade union and Borough Council weighed heavily on me. I felt deeply about many problems and, inevitably, when I took my seat on the Council I became involved in some stormy scenes. I had not been elected to condone slums and when I walked into the Council chamber for my first meeting I was determined to campaign for the people I represented. I found myself in a cosy and sedate atmosphere which discouraged vigorous debate. The whole chamber was flower-bedecked as if in floral homage to former Mayors whose portraits hung on the walls. Councillors sat around a polished, semi-circular table facing the Mayor, in his elevated chair, with aldermen on each side. Proceedings were formal, courteous and even pleasant. I resolved to toss a few stones into this tranquil political pond as soon as possible.

At the first opportunity I spoke of the urgent need for better houses and repairs to slums. My theme was simple, direct and important. Apart from the discomfort and misery caused by bad housing, the infantile mortality rate in my ward was ten per cent— more than twice as high as the national average of 4·5 per cent. This was mainly due to deplorable housing conditions and no one except the tenants seemed to be upset about it. When I protested, some members of the Council were uncertain about their attitude to me; although most Labour Councillors were friendly, the Conservatives treated my more outspoken attacks with disdain. In one debate a local Tory elder statesman said he strongly objected to my 'boy talk'. My rejoinders about 'living monuments of senility' hardly made for good relations with him and his colleagues, but enlivened the proceedings. People from my Ward came to listen to the debates with a growing awareness of their rights. I was accused of being repetitious by some councillors but it did not disturb me because I knew that it would take more than an isolated comment to improve houses and generate a new sense of urgency.

There were fewer acrimonious exchanges as I gradually established better relationships with fellow-councillors. In spite of hard-hitting debates, I sought to enlighten and persuade rather than to vilify and condemn. But I needed allies to back up my views and when one of the Council seats in my Ward became vacant a few months later I tried to get one of my supporters elected. Ken Merrifield, one of my closest friends, was gifted with a happy blend of integrity and humour: he was one of our shop stewards and although I felt he was rather old—he was about 30—I thought he would make a good Councillor.

We decided to fight a campaign similar to my own; Ken and I arranged to canvass every house in the Ward and speak at street corners. Our closest supporter was a Welshman named George Davies, who worked on the furnaces with us at Bolton's, and though his enthusiasm was limitless his capacity for public speaking was nil. He acted as chairman—with no chair—at street corner meetings. At work he would write out the most glittering introductions to Ken Merrifield and myself, then practise them by the furnaces. Bathed in its golden glow, elevated on a copper slab, he was Demosthenes personified. But before he addressed a street crowd he would perspire, take off his cap and say, 'Ladies and gentlemen, . . . Jack Ashley.'

At the end of a campaign lacking in sparkle, Ken Merrifield received fewer than 100 votes, much to the disgust of his wife, Nancy; on the gloomy walk back from the count she entertained us with a passionate diatribe about the lack of gratitude in politics. Nancy and Ken have been two of my closest and dearest friends. They have shared many joys and sorrows—that night was one of the sorrows.

Despite this setback, I continued to press for improved housing. My speeches were always fairly reported in the local *Weekly News* which was read by nearly everyone in Widnes. I became friends with the chief reporter, a small mild-mannered Scotsman who listened with understanding to my sometimes extravagant requests. As a result of my public work I was becoming well-known in the area, and so deeply involved in its problems that all my spare time was taken up with Council work and Trade Union responsibilities. I lived and worked in drab surroundings but I was happily absorbed in the battle to change them. Suddenly by chance the whole scene was transformed.

At work one day, as I waited in the garage for the meal break, I glanced through a newspaper and saw a report of scholarships to Oxford for working men. I showed it to a friend who agreed that it looked interesting, but we did not discuss it at length; I went home for lunch and promptly forgot all about it. A few days afterwards I thought about it again; I wondered if it might just be worth applying—but I had forgotten the name and address of the college in Oxford. Had my friend not remembered I should almost certainly never have applied and I might have stayed at Bolton's all my life. But he did remember. It was Ruskin College, Oxford, so I wrote to the Secretary asking for details. Apart from an essay, which I presume they wanted in order to prove that I was not wholly illiterate, the scholarship seemed to depend on an interview in Oxford at which practical experience and academic potential would be taken into account. Since I felt that academic potential was not my strong point I hoped my experience in local government and the trade union movement would be of some value.

While my application was being considered one of my Catholic friends, a teacher in Widnes, heard about it and asked me if I would like to go to the Catholic Workers' College in Oxford, although he knew that I was questioning my religious beliefs to the point of rejection. Perhaps he felt that a spell at a Catholic college would revive my flagging enthusiasm for the Church. I agreed to see the Principal, Father O'Shea, although I emphasised that I was not committing myself to go to the college even if invited.

Visiting Oxford was no great romantic experience for me. I took the train from Widnes and made straight for Ruskin College for an interview which turned out to be simply a pleasant conversation. I was not asked about any of the great national issues of the day, which was perhaps as well for I was completely bound up with the local problems of Widnes. I talked about my work and my hopes for the future; it all seemed friendly and civilised. I could not make up my mind if they were being open and frank, and a scholarship was easier than I had imagined, or if this was a kindly facade for a hopeless applicant. Later I went to see Father O'Shea at the Catholic Workers' College nearby. This gentle old man told me I would certainly be invited to enter the college if the Ruskin scholarship was not offered, though I received this news with some misgivings.

A few weeks later, as I walked home from the factory at lunch time, I saw my mother and my sister Helen waiting outside 34 Wellington Street. A letter had arrived from Oxford. I was now quite excited about the prospect and quickly opened it to find a message from Father O'Shea congratulating me on winning the Ruskin scholarship and regretting that I would not be joining him. I was delighted with the news but puzzled that the college had not yet officially informed me. After lunch my mother gave me a large envelope which she had put aside assuming it was some kind of advertisement; it was the official notification from Ruskin College that I had been awarded the scholarship. That letter marked the effective end of my life in industry and soon afterwards, in October 1946, I left the factory, gave up my official position in the Chemical Workers Union, and resigned from the Borough Council. My regret was mingled with excitement at the prospect of an entirely new life at Oxford.

6

Oxford

On the train to Oxford I noticed a small, dark man, chunkily built, who stood out from other student passengers. I could not define his quality but he interested me and I wondered if he, too, was going to Ruskin. Fortunately he was; we liked each other immediately and established a friendship which has continued to this day. A shipyard worker from Belfast, David Bleakley had a background similar to my own. A friend is particularly welcome in a new environment and on the short walk from station to college we agreed that if possible we would share a room.

The college was a relatively small building with a plain exterior. Scores of bicycles lined a passageway from the gate to a pleasant common room which was simply and tastefully furnished; newspapers and periodicals lay on comfortable settees and armchairs. The adjoining library looked well stocked and intimidating to me—a reminder of all the books I had not read. Across the hallway was a large lecture room and, on the floors above, the students' living quarters; the college was a neat and compact entity.

It had been opened, as Ruskin Hall, in 1899 and moved to its present site in 1903, where a new college was built ten years later. I assumed when I arrived that it was founded by Ruskin but oddly enough it was established on the initiative of two Americans. They admired Ruskin and, being interested in the Labour movement, decided to establish a college in Oxford to provide educational opportunities for working-class students. Although it did not become the centre of a national system of working-class colleges as they had hoped, the college itself survived. It had an eventful history, as we were to learn in the next few weeks; but that day our main concern was to find our way around new surroundings.

I liked the college, particularly the friendly and unaffected atmosphere, but felt disappointed that I would not live there until my second year. I left reluctantly—with David Bleakley—to go by bus to Headington, two miles outside Oxford, where we were to live for our first year. My mood changed when I saw 'The Rookery'—a spacious building with clean, white-painted woodwork, set in lovely meadows. It was purely residential, although there was a library for private study; lectures and tutorials took place at the college. David Bleakley and I moved from the separate rooms provisionally reserved for us into another shared by two students; one was a rather serious draughtsman and the other a tubby steelworker with the unlikely name of Claude.

During the evening we met the rest of the men with whom we were to share college life. Most of them had industrial experience similar to mine but there was a difference between us which I did not appreciate at the time. Although they were mainly manual workers such as miners, lorry drivers and shipyard workers, nearly all had taken courses of study before coming to Ruskin. Some were impressively well read though they had no academic qualifications. I had not studied at all since I left St Patrick's elementary school eight years earlier. All my work had been practical and time-consuming. The only books I had read were a handbook of regulations governing the Town Council and Jack London's *The Iron Heel*. I had found both interesting in their different ways but they were hardly an adequate preparation for a university diploma in Economics and Political Science.

The Principal, Lionel Elvin, had a deep understanding of students and I greatly admired him. He was my tutor in political science and when I stumbled through the intricacies of the political theories of Marx, Hobbes, Rousseau, Locke and T. H. Green, he marked my work frankly yet gave encouragement. I was rarely marked above B-plus, and often it was B, which was far from brilliant. But I always felt that Elvin, despite his own academic stature, appreciated the profound difficulties facing working-class students.

Every week I wrote a political essay which I discussed with him in an hour-long tutorial. He was an excellent teacher, genuinely interested in discussing ideas and persuading students to express their own. It was rather like boxing with a far superior opponent who wants to encourage you and will not take advantage of his greater skill. Yet he never patronised or pretended ignorance; he treated students as his equals in intelligence, if not in knowledge.

The Vice-Principal, Henry Smith, was a cherubic economist who stalked up and down the rostrum seeming to enjoy baffling students as he sprinkled lectures liberally with paradoxes. He was nevertheless a fine teacher, because his manner and enthusiasm immediately excited interest and having caught it he held it throughout.

Anyone who was unable to grasp a particular point would be invited to join him on a long walk to discuss the problem. I once accepted his invitation and found myself scurrying in the countryside around Oxford, trying to keep abreast of him and his erudite explanation of economic theory. I appreciated his kindness but I would have been wiser to stay in college with a book, learning the fundamentals before approaching him with more advanced problems.

It was impossible to keep up with one lecturer, a young constitutional historian; he was inexperienced and would recount as many facts, figures and dates as he could within the hour. Even at St Patrick's I had mentally switched off at the mention of the names of monarchs, the dates of their reigns, and the details of their births, marriages and deaths. At Oxford I made just as little effort to absorb this bombardment of information, which I still found uninteresting and irrelevant.

One other noteworthy teacher was the social history tutor, Stephen Schofield. Resembling Malcolm Muggeridge in both appearance and manner, he spoke slowly and reflectively but his urbane manner was part of a ploy to shock students by debunking historical myths. 'The Peterloo Massacre?' he would ask innocently, extending his arms widely. 'But only a few old men and a dog were killed that day, so I don't know why they call it a massacre.' He was one of the most interesting and amusing lecturers in Oxford and we enjoyed his performance.

Although Ruskin was not part of the university we were able to attend lectures and use the libraries. Lectures in Ruskin were instructive but relaxed occasions, conducted by men whom we came to know well. By comparison, university lectures were formal affairs and most dons seemed remote and impersonal. It was in the university lecture halls and reading rooms that I was most acutely aware of the differences between Ruskin students and undergraduates. They wore gowns and we did not, but the differences went deeper than that. Starkly contrasting backgrounds were reflected not only in clothes but in our attitudes to society. Not every undergraduate was an irresponsible dilettante nor every Ruskin man a responsible, thoughtful citizen, but the university men seemed to possess a boyish bonhomie, or even flippancy, that was not shared by students at Ruskin.

Their accents were different from ours, reflecting long established class divisions in British society. Our backgrounds in factories, mines and shipyards were not easily suited to academic disciplines and we were surprised to find ourselves at Oxford. They seemed settled in their natural habitat and fitted in snugly—we sometimes thought smugly—with the cloisters and spires. The impression may have been false but it was powerful—and prevented me from ever feeling completely at home in Oxford. I felt impoverished in comparison with some undergraduates, a few of whom flaunted their extravagance. As I was sending part of my allowance to my mother I had great difficulty in managing.

I was so short of money that I answered the advertisement of an old middle-class couple who wanted a girl to clean their house. They were astonished when I applied, but as no girls volunteered they accepted me. Three or four times a week I went to clean their living room, bring coal in from a shed in the garden and light the fire at about four o'clock. It was a far cry from the tough, rumbustious atmosphere of the factory where I had loaded furnaces; as I kindled the little fire I felt lonely and gloomy. They were a genteel old couple, who retired to bed after lunch and came down later for afternoon tea. They were grateful for my work but I disliked it, feeling that I was misusing my time.

I had to find money from somewhere, so I wrote to my Member of Parliament, Christopher Shawcross, for a further education grant. The condition of such a grant was that an educational course broken by war service was being resumed. Imagination was needed to see myself as a scholar before I left Bolton's but I convinced myself with platitudes about learning in the universities of industry and life. A generous Minister of Education, giving me the benefit of what must have been monumental doubt, awarded me the grant. It meant leaving the old couple, but I felt so sorry for them that I kept extending my notice to quit until they found someone else.

Whatever the problems, Ruskin students never allowed them to stifle their sense of humour; lessons and social life were enlivened by their wit. Our occasional concerts were memorable for their satire. Once a tutor's lecturing eccentricities were caricatured so perceptively and devastatingly that he changed his style—for a few days. David Bleakley and I, at the age of 22, were two of the youngest students in Ruskin and we took part in the fun. On one occasion, in a flippant mood, he rang the dinner bell half an hour early. We joined the puzzled queue, agreeing with irate students that it was odd for an early call to be followed by a long delay.

In addition to his sense of humour David soon showed his

strength of character. With his Irish brogue he was once referred to as 'Paddy'. He mentioned, apparently casually, that his name was David, but when he was called Paddy again he icily informed the offender, 'I've already told you my name is David, not Paddy. If you can't understand that I'm prepared to repeat it for you until you do.' Never again was he addressed by the name which conjures up a picture of an Irish peasant. One of the most gifted students, he was quite untroubled by the work. But I found none of it easy and it took me a long time to master the basic elements of the course.

I realised somewhat belatedly that it was essential to study in the first few months or one was left behind and could never quite catch up with a subject. Lecturers would go ahead on the assumption that the preceding lesson had been understood. My greatest mistake at Oxford was failing to grasp the essentials of the work in those early days. Ploughing through Marshall's vast tract on the *Principles of Economics* tested me sorely; it did not help when others praised its simplicity and lucidity. The other students were soon discussing the subtleties of the theories of marginal utility but it remained a vague notion in my mind far too long.

I was much happier with political theory. Although I was impatient to study current controversies, rather than the ancient ones of Plato, Aristotle and Socrates, I appreciated that these gave philosophical depth and understanding to fundamental political problems of all times. Later we moved on to the theories of more modern political thinkers and argued about them between ourselves. Some Ruskin students were dedicated Marxists but I found the philosophy unacceptable. Despite my past conflicts with employers, I did not agree with much of Marx—and certainly not his theory of the inevitability of a working-class uprising against the bourgeoisie. I had a firm preference for democratic, rather than revolutionary, change.

By this time I had become a strong Labour Party supporter. I had always been anti-Conservative on class grounds as they clearly supported privilege. In Widnes they favoured employers and landlords against trade unionists and tenants—to me they were natural opponents. My studies at Ruskin provided theoretical justification for my socialist instincts. I learned to appreciate the historical significance of the Labour Movement and my differences with the Labour Party, caused by my association with the ILP and conflict with local Councillors, fell into perspective.

At Ruskin I saw, for the first time, direct clashes between the social democrats of the Labour Party and the revolutionaries of the Communist Party. The Communists were assertive and dogmatic, expressing their opinions in political jargon. They patronised the social democrats. Nothing pains a radical more than to be told he is only a milk-and-water reformer, lacking the rich red blood of a man of action. The revolutionary fervour was so much in evidence in my early days at Ruskin that I felt almost apologetic for being a social democrat—but I soon learned to stop that.

Personal friendships survived political differences though extreme views could disturb a relationship. I went to an Oxford bookshop with a friend who held deep Communist convictions. We selected our books and were about to return to college when, instead of going to the till to pay, he left by a side door. When I later asked him if he had stolen the books he told me not to be so naive. He explained that printers and publishers were making vast profits by exploiting the workers; they were unjustly supported by laws made by the ruling class so his action was a justifiable retaliation. Arguments about morality, the rule of law and the ends not justifying the means left him totally unmoved. I liked him and avoided using another argument—that his theory was simply a rationalisation of a selfish action—because he was basically a considerate person, but I felt I could never fully trust him afterwards.

I enjoyed my first year at Ruskin, particularly the companionship of other students, but I could not claim to have made great academic progress. I did not take to study easily, preferring practical politics to theoretical, and I lacked intellectual discipline. Few students are ever satisfied with their studies at college—most bemoan the work they have not done, and I was no exception.

At the end of the year, in June 1947, I returned to Widnes for the long summer vacation. Despite my gratitude to Ruskin for the educational opportunity, I soon put my books aside and resumed my fight for better housing. This time, instead of acting on my own, I went to see the local Labour Councillors. They were willing to cooperate and called a special meeting in St Patrick's church hall to shake up the authorities.

At this crowded meeting the Councillors spoke first and I was about to make the final speech when the lights went out. No one knew whether it was an electrical failure or, as we suspected, sabotage, but before long some candles were produced. In this peculiar setting, amid flickering candlelight, I made an emotional speech quoting the high death rate of babies and condemning the landlords as having 'blood on their hands'. The audience was aroused and disturbed, many of the women being deeply moved. I promised to amass the evidence and seek urgent action from the Council.

Pursuing this campaign did not further my Oxford career. Three months' reading would have helped my studies considerably, but after only a few days at home I felt as if I had never been away. Oxford seemed distant and irrelevant and I was happier resuming my campaigning. In the next few months I visited hundreds of homes, collecting evidence of appalling conditions in the town—cases of gross over-crowding and of people who were ill living in slums which aggravated their illnesses. Scarce building materials were being used to repair and renovate cinemas and football grounds while houses were neglected. I also sought to show that new Council houses had not been allocated to those in greatest need.

When I completed the evidence I told the Town Clerk, who invited me to appear before a special joint meeting of the Health and Housing Committee of the Council. He warned that there would be a verbatim report of my speech, with a possible legal action if I slandered anyone. The Committees had obviously decided to give me enough rope to hang myself and, apart from one or two pointed questions by the Town Clerk, there was no discussion. Eventually all my demands for an enquiry were rejected but my efforts were not in vain. There was no doubt that the number of housing repairs and the allocation of Council houses were significantly affected by the campaign.

The Town Clerk behaved impeccably throughout. A thin man with an incisive manner, he would peer through his spectacles and say, rather primly, 'May I remind you, Mr Ashley, of the Standing Orders of the Council concerning the point that you seek to raise.' Yet this formal exterior disguised a deep humanity. He told me after the meeting that when he read the evidence again he was impressed by the presentation. He may have been but I heard that he spoke against all my demands, as he warned me he would do. But I knew that he was sympathetic. Although he had no option but to defend the Council's policy, he did all he could to help those in need. His opposition did not alter my profound and abiding friendship for him and I always appreciated the guidance he gave me. I was deeply saddened by his death a few years afterwards in a car crash.

When I returned to Oxford for my second year I lived in the college and intensified my studies. Now there was a new intake at 'The Rookery' and we, as the seniors, were expected to know our economics and political science. As the year progressed the examinations began to loom large, and inevitably this was reflected in our conversation. The subjects we were studying became a more frequent topic. It was an interesting, if subtle, difference from the early days at Ruskin. At 'The Rookery' we were a diverse collection of individuals taking a course of study, whereas in the college we were a corporate body of students approaching a searching test. Not only was our personal standing involved but also the reputation of the college; it had provided us with time, opportunity, books, lectures and tuition. If many failed we would let down the college as well as ourselves. I was by no means confident since examinations were wholly unfamiliar to me, as they were to many Ruskin students. Having no method of assessing my standard, and keenly aware of my lack of earlier study, I went apprehensively for my diploma exams.

The tension must have been tremendous because when I walked out of the examination hall after the final paper Oxford looked different to me. The sun shone and the spires glittered more brightly than they ever had before. It was all over—no more anxiety and intensive studying for me. That night I celebrated with my friends and we happily agreed that there was no point now in worrying about the results. What was done was done. All we could do was sit back and wait. But then someone mentioned that many Ruskin students were applying for the two extra-mural scholarships to Oxford University, the two to Cambridge University, and ten available State scholarships. I joined the throng, thinking that in the unlikely event of being successful I would then decide whether to accept.

The first stage of the examination was a written essay on any subject we chose. I decided on an imaginary conversation between T. H. Green, the Social Democrat, and Karl Marx. Although I was fairly familiar with the political views of both, I spent a few weeks intently studying their works. It was strange that I should find myself totally absorbed and enjoying deep study only at the end of my two years in Oxford and I regretted that I had left it so late. This was not the fault of the college—it was due to my background and temperament. I took special care with the essay, which reflected the clash of philosophy and political theory between these two men who naturally debated the most profound political issues—but I felt that I needed a lighter ending. Marx concluded by saying that they did not seem to have got very far in the discussion. 'No,' said Green, 'but if only it has enabled this bright young man to get a scholarship to Cambridge, surely it will have been well worthwhile.' Despite this cheeky ending my essay secured me a place on the short list for all of the scholarships—Oxford, Cambridge and the State.

Two other Ruskin students, David Bleakley and Eric Linfield, were also short-listed for the Cambridge scholarship and the three of us travelled together for the interview. No doubt the others were wondering, as I was, which of us might be successful and which would be disappointed. No one spoke about this on the journey, but in Cambridge, as we were walking by Fenner's playing field, David Bleakley put my thoughts into words when he said, 'I wonder whether this will be our first and last time in Cambridge or if it will become familiar to any of us in the next three years.'

We were interviewed in turn by the Board; they questioned me about the essay, my background and my hopes for the future. They were informal and friendly with all of us so there was no realistic way of assessing the impression each had made. But the following morning at breakfast in Ruskin I was congratulated by a smiling student who had just heard that the college had carried off both Cambridge scholarships and that Eric Linfield and I were the successful candidates. I was delighted for I had taken an immediate and instinctive liking to Cambridge. Lionel Elvin, himself a Cambridge man, came to congratulate me and we had a celebratory drink.

I was allocated a place at Gonville and Caius College. When I met my tutor, Stanley Dennison, I took to him immediately although I knew our values were very different. I still had a lurking doubt about passing the Oxford diploma examination so I asked him what would happen if I failed. He assured me that it would make no difference and that my Cambridge scholarship was safe regardless of the Oxford results. When they were published I was pleased, and somewhat relieved, to find that I had passed. It was no surprise to anyone, least of all to me, that David Bleakley passed with a

Distinction and I wondered if that result would have affected the Cambridge scholarship decision had it been known at the time. But within weeks he won a scholarship to Queen's University, Belfast. Later he became Minister for Community Relations in Northern Ireland—undoubtedly a prelude to an outstanding political career.

In my final few weeks at Oxford, before the long summer break in Widnes, I became involved in another public controversy. I received a copy of the *Weekly News* every week and I read a report of a speech by the leader of the Conservative group on the Widnes Council, Dr Baxter, a senior ICI chemist who later became a professor at Sydney University. He had suggested that the trade unions should end their affiliation with the Labour Party and become politically independent. The subject interested me since I was convinced of the need for unity between the two wings of the Labour movement. I challenged Dr Baxter to a public debate and he accepted. This created great interest in the town and the Trades Council offered to make the arrangements under the chairmanship of the Town Clerk.

I began studying history books for all the relevant Acts and significant dates and soon compiled an imposing array. Just before I left Ruskin for Widnes I met Stephen Schofield, the social history tutor, and told him about the forthcoming debate. He was agreeably interested and I was encouraged enough to show him my imposing list of data. Glancing through them he said to me with a slow smile, 'I'd chuck 'em away if I were you. All you need is three or four points. And debate, don't recite.' His advice rang true. After very little reflection I did as he suggested but I took the precaution of seeking from the Conservative Central Office their views about the relationship between the trade unions and the Labour Party. Their reply, prompt and comprehensive, enabled me to study at leisure my opponent's case for what was to be the first formal public debate of my life.

Even some of my warmest supporters in Widnes felt I had bitten off more than I could chew. The most that Ken Merrifield would allow himself to say was, 'Well, he's a very clever man, you know.' This, coming from a close friend, was a little ominous. We walked to the debate together, ostensibly exuding confidence though I was beginning to share his qualms. The debate had attracted wide attention and hundreds of people were swarming into the hall as we approached; I noted with dismay that many of them had come in cars from the more prosperous parts of the town.

I spoke first, and although my speech was well received I thought Dr Baxter's was better. I was relieved that he followed exactly the lines I had anticipated so that when I replied to the debate I was able to quote the sources of his quotations, and even some of his phrases; then I subjected them to a barrage of what I hoped was withering criticism. The Town Clerk took a vote by a show of hands. It was evident that I had won by a wide margin but he diplomatically announced 'a narrow majority' for me. Of course the vote was meaningless, because I noticed that my people voted solidly for me and Dr Baxter's supporters voted without exception for him. As the hall was overcrowded, it was really a question of whose supporters had arrived first and were able to cast their votes within sight of the chairman while those in the corridors went unseen.

Nevertheless I was delighted with the result—the occasion whetted my appetite for debate, and it was to influence my activities at Cambridge.

7

Cambridge

On my first day at Cambridge I felt a sense of exhilaration which lasted throughout my stay. Although I had been happy at Ruskin I never loved Oxford; its atmosphere, which many students found heady or inspiring, did not affect me deeply. Yet I was captivated by Cambridge, where few things ever quenched my exuberant spirits—and never any of them for long. I did not feel the same jolting sense of sudden shunting from factory to college as at Oxford; now I was a full member of the university, acclimatised to an academic atmosphere.

Many of the colleges are very old and my own, Gonville and Caius, founded in 1348, is one of the oldest. An attractive modern block faces the busy market square, but it is the older buildings, surrounding neat quadrangles with a lovely chapel as the centre-piece, which create the studious atmosphere. The college is ideally placed, with wide-sweeping King's Parade on one side and the languorous, tree-lined river Cam behind it.

In 1948, the mixture of students was particularly interesting. Some had come straight from school, many had completed their two years' national service and a few of the older ones had been in the forces during the war. Most were middle-class, and there was a good sprinkling of public school boys—with accents to match.

In my college there were no workers or factory labourers to provide instant companionship. At the first formal assembly for freshmen many students seemed to know each other, and they grouped together with a buzz of animated chatter. No one spoke to me and although I made a few attempts at light conversation they soon faded. Yet I did not feel uncomfortable. I looked forward to my years with this cheerful crowd, knowing that our class and backgrounds were different but not expecting them to cause any serious problems.

I had heard about college servants, known as scouts, who looked after students, and addressed them as 'Sir'. Perhaps they were some kind of civilian batmen, waiting hand and foot on busy under-graduates? My scout turned out to be a middle-aged woman whose job was to clean and tidy the rooms; she called me 'Sir', but in a wholly unaffected and friendly way, accepting it as part of the normal verbal currency. In her attitude, entirely without deference, she displayed a sense of humour which would have demolished any idea of a personal 'batman'.

I was allocated attractive rooms in the forecourt—a sitting room and an adjoining bedroom—to be shared with a fellow student. Another David Bleakley, perhaps? But when he entered I knew that we shared nothing in common, except unease in each other's company; it was not just a difference of class or character but a disturbing combination of both. He was tall, elegant and self-assured, with an upper-class accent—when he spoke at all. No doubt he resented a rough, working-class character sharing his rooms. Either the authorities had an odd sense of humour or they calculated that I could gain, and he could lose, a little polish to our mutual advantage.

I expected the relationship to improve when we got to know each other, but for some months we lived together without a spark of friendship. Attitudes were partly motivated by pride in our class and backgrounds, though discord was muted by his impeccable manners. Even the small gestures at mutual accommodation seemed to emphasise rather than soften our differences. One day he received a parcel from his mother containing Stilton cheese, which I had never seen before. When he offered me some I cut a hefty chunk, rather like hacking a piece of Cheddar in the factory canteen, and made a sandwich. He murmured that the best way to enjoy Stilton was to eat a little at a time. Remarkably enough, we did become friends—eventually.

Despite the uneasy months with my room-mate I never found class alone prevented friendships. Some of the few working-class students at Cambridge felt bitter about class and the inequality it reflected. But I did not share their bitterness although I knew that many middle- and upper-class students enjoyed, and took for granted, wealth and privilege unknown in Widnes. If some students had cut-glass accents they were as much the product of their environment as my Lancashire accent was of mine. I was not inclined to allow my firm political opposition to class privilege to degenerate into personal vendettas.

Nevertheless financial differences could occasionally create awkward situations, as I soon learned. One night as we walked down-

stairs from the dining hall a group of friendly students invited me
to have a drink at the 'buttery'. This turned out to be a small
shop below the dining room which sold wines and spirits, but I
had not noticed it before.

'What will you have—a glass of port?'

'Well—yes, certainly,' I replied, reflecting that port wine was
something we had with mince pies at Christmas in Widnes.

It was a pleasant drink and an enjoyable conversation, although
later, when I bought a round of drinks for the group, I was stunned
at the cost. Apart from special occasions I kept away from the
'buttery' after that.

Of course many pleasures at university cost nothing; especially
those which were simple or evocative. Curiously enough, listening
to the college bell calling students to dinner greatly pleased me;
the pealing or tolling of bells has always affected me and this was
no exception. As a child in Wellington Street on tranquil Sunday
afternoons I used to listen with pleasure to the church bells pealing
in the Town Hall Square a quarter of a mile away. The bells of
St Patrick's church, just before Mass, were a solemn and welcome
call to duty. In Caius College the bell was rung for five minutes
before the evening meal as gowned students and tutors made their
way across the quadrangle to the dining hall. Somehow this bell
symbolised for me the traditions and academic spirit of Cambridge
more than all the buildings.

In hall we stood in long lines at the tables; when the bell stopped
silence fell—to be broken by the intoning of a Latin prayer from
the high table. I sometimes wondered, as I stood with bowed head,
what my friends in Widnes would be doing at that moment—and
what robust and irreverent comments they would have made if they
could have seen me.

No one had any real excuse for not working at Cambridge. The
way of life was organised to ensure maximum opportunity for study;
we had our own college rooms, splendid libraries and regular daily
lectures. Although there was no compulsion to attend lectures, I
was encouraged by my tutor to go and listen to the many world-
famous economists who taught in Cambridge. Each lecture started
punctually on the hour and finished a few minutes before the next,
so that students rushed from one lecture room to the other. I rushed
a little more than most to get a front seat as I could not hear clearly
if I sat at the back.

It was interesting to see how the individual characteristics of the lecturers emerged. In the economics faculty Professor Robertson was sardonic and witty; Joan Robinson authoritative and clear; Stanley Dennison intellectual and informative. I liked Dennison very much. A dark, handsome man with aquiline features and a gentle voice, he was my tutor in college and each week I spent an hour with him discussing my essay on economics. In dealing with social economic affairs it is difficult to draw an exact line between economic theory and political argument. Dennison encouraged me to analyse my own assumptions and was prepared to discuss his own without attempting to persuade me to accept them.

In the first few weeks I visited various university clubs and sporting groups where some of the games were unfamiliar to me. I had never played tennis before and did rather badly; at squash I was quick but unskilled; when I tried rowing I became bored. I was quite fast and strong, with swift reflexes, and I decided I should try my old game, rugby. The first College game was a sort of Probables versus Possibles and I went along to play. Unfortunately the referee did not arrive and, since no one seemed to want the job, I volunteered. I was an expert at this game, having played Rugby League often in Widnes, and I knew the rules well. Soon after the game started the ball was kicked ahead over the touchline without first bouncing inside. This meant no ground was gained and I ordered the teams back to the kicking point; they were obviously astonished, but obeyed my instructions. Next time this happened the man who kicked the ball tried to argue with me but I dismissed this as bad sportsmanship. Gradually I felt a sense of incredulity spreading among both teams.

I assumed that the rules of Rugby Union in Cambridge were the same as those of Rugby League in Widnes—but they were not! Before long the teams were playing to their own rules by common consent; players would stop without my whistle or go on in spite of it. It must have been the first time in the history of the college that two teams worked in such harmony with total disregard of a referee. The comments I overheard later were hardly complimentary; it was clear that I should confine my football activities to Rugby League.

When I joined the University Labour Club I anticipated differences between university politics and local government. In Widnes the arguments were about practical problems whereas in Cambridge

they were purely theoretical. It was difficult to take solemnly, although many people did, but I took an active part in the Club's
affairs. We had business meetings and discussions during the week
and a visiting speaker at the weekend. These were the liveliest
meetings, when we pitted our wits against Members of Parliament
or any others who had a political view to express. I enjoyed all
these activities and was elected chairman before the end of my
first year.

Some of the leaders of the Labour and Conservative Clubs were
interesting personalities. The Conservatives were led by men like
Norman St John Stevas and Geoffrey Howe, who later became
Members of Parliament. St John Stevas was a skilled satirist and
a fine debater; I liked him despite his apparent eccentricities. His
dress was often formal and sometimes foppish but he was brave
enough to wear it regardless of the jests of friends and the taunts
of foes. Howe was quiet, painstaking and serious, and while St John
Stevas became the President of the Cambridge Union Debating
Society, Howe rose no further than being a member of the Committee. Yet he was to race effortlessly ahead of all his contempor-
aries. Immediately after the Conservatives regained power in 1970, he
became Solicitor-General and, soon afterwards, a Cabinet Minister.

The Union Society was generally regarded as a training ground
for budding politicians. Yet Howe's success in the Commons seems
to indicate that Parliament requires qualities different from or
additional to those demanded of a Union President. Debating skill
is useful in government, but while it may be an end in itself in the
Union far more is required of a first-class Minister.

Among the leaders of the Labour Club were two remarkable
personalities: Percy Craddock and Bill Wedderburn. Craddock was
an outstanding Cambridge figure, whose brilliance was widely
acknowledged. He had a distinguished academic record—with
starred Firsts in English and Law. Eloquent, yet never taking
himself too seriously, he dazzled the Labour Club and Union
Society. He was sensitive and fastidious and I felt that his wit was a
defensive rapier guarding a gentle man. It seemed in character that
he was interested in ancient Chinese civilisation. He became one
of our leading diplomats in Peking and later entered the Cabinet
Office.

Bill Wedderburn was also a lawyer with a starred First: he was
the first law student for some ten years to win the Chancellor's law

[83]

medal. Although never President of the Union, he was a commanding orator and a significant figure in the political life of Cambridge.
Twenty years later, as a professor of industrial law, he was relied
upon by the whole Labour movement in Britain for legal advice
in the fight against the Industrial Relations Bill—which was master-
minded by Sir Geoffrey Howe.

The first clash between members of opposing political clubs I
witnessed at the Union Society was a sparkling occasion. Its setting
was novel to me; the chamber, modelled on the House of Commons,
was crowded with eager students. Precisely on time, the President
and officers, all in evening dress, escorted the guest speakers to
their seats. At a single ping from the President's bell the students
fell silent and listened to the terms of the motion—then battle com-
menced. The opening speech by a Conservative student, quite
impressive in both content and delivery, was enthusiastically received and I did not envy the following speaker. But it was the
eloquent Craddock, who trumped every ace with wit and debating
skill. I resolved that night to join the Union Society, a decision
that gave me pleasure throughout my years at Cambridge.

Shortly afterwards I made my first speech in a debate on Ireland,
initiated by De Valera. I didn't know a great deal about the intricacies of the Irish question but this did not deter me. My speech
was fairly well received but I knew that I could do better with more
familiar subjects. A few weeks later Percy Craddock told me that
I would shortly receive an invitation from the President to be one
of the two main speakers in a forthcoming debate. I hoped for a
political subject but Craddock said the motion was to be 'The
scientist and the artist must accept responsibility for the social
consequences of their work'. He looked at me wryly when I asked
him who my opponent was to be, and admitted, with a smile, that
he was.

I had never thought about the subject; when I did, the question
of an artist's responsibility baffled me. Obviously this was an ab-
struse problem deserving careful study so I headed for the university
library where I was offered a pile of books which might be relevant,
although the library assistant was doubtful. The doubt was justified;
I left with an empty notebook after studying for hours. In the
debate I devoted a little of my time to jocular criticism of the
President for his choice of motion and for saddling me with the
responsibility of dealing with it. This was received better than any

erudite passage about artistic responsibility, but the debate was notable for yet another eloquent contribution from Craddock.

I attended the Union Society regularly throughout my first year and spoke as often as I could although never as frequently as I wished. There were always more people trying to speak than the time allowed. Yet I could not complain, because I had many opportunities, especially when I became chairman of the Labour Club. In my second year I was elected to the Union Committee and a few terms later, I headed the poll and became the senior member.

The next stage was to stand for the Secretaryship. My opponent was Tony Bullock, an intelligent and able Conservative, and although I just managed to beat him my term as Secretary aroused some controversy. Just before the election, *Varsity*, the undergraduate newspaper, published a profile of me which my opponents claimed influenced the result. To make matters worse, I continued to wear a lounge suit after I was elected, despite the long-standing tradition that evening dress should be worn by the three officers of the Society. My action should have been no surprise to anyone as I had made my intention quite clear before the election. I was not standing on any great principle—I simply couldn't afford an evening suit and I had no intention of hiring one. I was incredulous that there should be such concern over my clothes but they became an important issue when I stood for the Vice-Presidency.

Shortly before the election a pointed personal attack on me was printed in the Oxford *Isis*. The anonymous critic wrote: 'No one would object to an officer appearing at debates in a lounge suit through financial necessity, but to do so (as no other officers who were Socialists have done) on account of perverted political principle seems to many to amount to a gratuitous insult to the dignity of his office.' The article, timely for my opponents, was given much publicity in Cambridge. My natural reaction was to fire off a strong rejoinder, but I was dissuaded by two of my colleagues, Percy Craddock and a Jewish mathematician, Ivor Robinson, who were generally regarded as the elder statesmen of the Labour Club. They were to be the diplomatists and professors of a decade later and they displayed their talents with the advice they offered. Instead of an angry retort, I made a restrained reply saying that I was sorry that so violent a personal attack should have been launched upon me in an election which, I had hoped, would have been conducted along very different lines. I never knew whether my reply was effective or if the original attack backfired. Perhaps it was regarded as irrelevant by members of the Union; in any case I won the Vice-Presidency and with a comfortable majority of over ninety. The following term I was returned unopposed as President.

Despite my years in the slums and factories of Widnes I felt completely at ease in the Union and enjoyed my term of office. I was the first working-class President of the Society, which was predominantly middle-class with a sprinkling of aristocrats. Their experience and values were different from mine—not better or worse, but different. Yet I moved as easily and comfortably among them as with my friends in Wellington Street. I didn't change them, and looking back I can see that they never changed me.

The selection of subjects, guest speakers and student contributors for the debates were my first main tasks. The weekly debates were the centrepiece around which the Society's activities revolved. Formal yet lively occasions, they were preceded by dinner with the main guests and speakers. These were the first official dinners of my life and I found them interesting affairs; the food and service were excellent, but two things surprised me: the formal atmosphere soon became convivial and the port and brandy moved around the table with impressively casual precision.

My guests included such contrasting characters as Selwyn Lloyd, Gilbert Harding, Hugh Dalton, Godfrey Winn, Donald Soper and Jeremy Thorpe—although, of course, some care was exercised in pitting one against another. Inviting a politician with a comedian, no matter how attractive a proposition, would have been a recipe for disaster. Two people I thought would make good opponents in a debate on world peace were my friend Bob Edwards of the Chemical Workers' Union and Randolph Churchill.

Although Edwards was a fine conference orator, the Union Society was not the place for his particular talents and he did not really adapt himself. His speech, which would have electrified a political conference, was received with some banter by unimpressed though friendly students. As he was speaking of the horrors of war Churchill baited him by waving his handkerchief as the white flag of surrender; in fact Edwards was no pacifist, having fought bravely in the Spanish Civil War. But the scene is etched in my mind as an example of misplaced oratory on the one hand and the caricature of it by Churchill on the other.

Near the end of my Presidential term I was invited to make a debating tour of United States universities, along with Ronald Waterhouse, my predecessor. He was a tall, well-groomed Liberal lawyer who came from a middle-class home. Although our backgrounds were different we were friends who greatly enjoyed each other's company. We lightly agreed to speak on any of six motions which were sent to twenty American universities—each choosing the one it preferred. The two most provocative motions were that we 'deplored the banning of Communist parties in free, democratic states' and that we 'regretted the American way of life'. These were the two most popular subjects although one of the others— 'that Democratic Socialism is the most effective barrier against Soviet Communism'—was chosen by a few universities. We combined on the first two issues and opposed each other on the last one.

I was to be away for six weeks and my final examinations were due within a month of my return from America so I took a case full of books on the journey. The tour was so hectic that the case was never opened; I had simply given myself an added burden to carry around the States. Because of the pressure of time, neither Waterhouse nor I had prepared speeches on any of the six subjects when we embarked on the Queen Elizabeth but we intended to work on them during the voyage. However the entertainments on the ship, together with the excitement of a first trip to the United States, induced us to enjoy a frivolously gay voyage. When the ship berthed in New York we took stock of the situation—a tour of twenty universities beginning next day, a journey from the Atlantic to the Pacific, and no speeches prepared.

Our first debate was at St Joseph's College, Philadelphia; I expected it to take a similar form to our own in Cambridge though perhaps in a more modern building. We were accustomed to speaking in a small debating chamber, with our audience around us, interjecting at will in the debate. At Philadelphia there was no audience participation in this sense, although they listened intently. Instead we were perched, with our opponents, on a stage in a vast stadium—the Union Jack draped behind us, the Stars and Stripes behind them—and facing us were 3,000 people. The event had been advertised as an international debate, adjudicated by a distinguished panel of judges which included a Federal Court judge, a Congressman, a professor and the president of an insurance company; the British Consul turned out to give us moral support which, in the circumstances, we appreciated.

Doubtless the organisers intended it to be a serious occasion but Cambridge debates were often liberally spiced with humour and we decided not to change our style. The audience readily responded although I suspect they were laughing at our accents more than our wit. The American team were more solemn, adopting a formal pattern we were to recognise throughout the tour—introduction, facts, interpretation of facts, conclusion and peroration. This rigidity made our opponents predictable targets and we took full advantage.

The Americans treated us like visiting celebrities. After the debate, a crowd of teenagers asked for autographs before we went to a late night party. Exhausted, we were rushed off to Ohio, the first taste of a rigorous schedule which was to take us to the Pacific coast and back. During the next few weeks we accepted warm American hospitality while maintaining in debates that we deplored their way of life. But they were tolerant and generous hosts.

We were often puzzled that a comment which was well received at one university would be greeted with relative silence in another. The main reason was probably the geographical and local differences which we learned to appreciate as we travelled across the continent. Waterhouse capitalised on local jealousy with great aplomb. He had heard of the keen competition between the University of Southern California (USC) and the University of California at Los Angeles (UCLA). When he was introduced at USC he coolly, and apparently mistakenly and fulsomely, said what a great privilege it was on that occasion to address the best university in California—UCLA. People gasped as he eulogised the other university, hardly knowing whether to be embarrassed or angry. He worked the trick in reverse just as effectively when we debated at UCLA.

Some of the debates were at girls' colleges and we were intrigued by our welcome. On arrival we would be met by the Headmistress and Head Girl who escorted us to the dining hall where hundreds of girls waited. Bright and fresh, dressed in a riot of colour, they would sing for us before dinner. It was difficult to be gallant in the debate which followed because we merely sounded ineffective or patronising or both, but the real test was still to come. Waterhouse and I were placed at opposite ends of a large common room and the girls gathered round in two groups to question us about England.

It was natural that the debonair Waterhouse should attract a majority of the girls, but during the discussions they tended to wander from his group to mine. Just before the final debate at a girls' college he jocularly threatened me that he would win and hold the largest crowd. It did not work out that way, but at the end of the evening he discovered the reason; while he had been intelligently discussing some of the economic and political problems facing Britain, I had been talking about the love life of the average English male.

We debated on the journey back to the east coast and at the end of the tour we were weary but hoped to resume studying for exams on the return voyage. I achieved very little and arrived back in Cambridge to find that most students were revising ground I had not even touched on. It was near the end of April and I had to take my exams in less than a month. One of my friends, who agreed to outline the lectures he had attended in my absence, brought his notes to my room. We were interrupted by a Girton undergraduate who was helping on the University newspaper *Varsity*—a lovely girl with dark brown hair and light blue eyes. She wanted to ask me about the debating tour, but it was out of the question at that moment. I asked her to return the following day, but she could not and offered to ask the editor to send someone else. I told her that since this was the first time *Varsity* had ever sent me a pretty reporter, if she would not interview me no one else could. She accepted the compliment and came back the next day.

I was more interested in the girl than the interview so we chatted about amusing incidents of the tour. Waterhouse had talked to her at some length about the USA but when her report appeared his views were more or less neglected; I joked about it when we met and warned him not to be too critical as I was now going out with the girl, Pauline Crispin. It was as well that I did, because at the end of the year he was a guest at our wedding.

My final examinations shortly afterwards were rather an ordeal. I was remorseful at neglecting my studies—no doubt a feeling shared by many undergraduates. But I was relieved to leave Cambridge with a second-class Honours Degree and in June 1951 I set about finding a job in the trade union movement from whence I came.

8

Labouring—and the Lost Election

As a result of a misunderstanding, I returned to Widnes with an Oxford diploma, a Cambridge degree and no job. Although I had not been promised a post in the Chemical Workers' Union, Bob Edwards had talked about the possibility of my becoming his assistant. No doubt he was thinking aloud and speculating, but I unwisely assumed there would be a job waiting when I left Cambridge: but I was mistaken. As I was anxious to work in the Labour movement I got in touch with George Woodcock, then assistant General Secretary of the Trades Union Congress, who suggested I should approach individual trade union leaders. He offered to speak to Tom Williamson, leader of the giant National Union of General and Municipal Workers. This was the union I had fought when I organised the Chemical Workers' Union at Bolton's, but Woodcock spoke highly of Williamson and felt he might have a job for me. I wrote to him but I was not very hopeful.

Meanwhile I needed a temporary job as my scholarship grant had ended and I had no money. Once again I was living with my mother, whom I was anxious to help—and I was planning to get married at the end of the year. I applied to the Corporation building department, where I had been given temporary labouring jobs during two long vacations, and they took me on once again. My brief periods with them had been happy interludes between studies at university. I worked with two old friends who were strikingly different in physique, character and outlook—yet they shared fun and laughter which made light of heavy work.

Tom Cosgrove looked like a bull-necked prizefighter; of medium height, he was barrel-chested and stocky, with powerful arms and shoulders. When I tried to wrestle with him, and I was no weakling, he would simply lift me off my feet and hold me in the air. We had been close friends since the days when he had been one of the shop stewards at Bolton's, and we enjoyed working together. He worked hard and expected others to do the same, though few could keep up with him physically when the pressure was on—but our other workmate was a man who loved to loaf.

A small, thin man named Billy, he devoted most of his time to avoiding work; he seemed to be one of the downtrodden characters of this world—a kind of Charlie Chaplin figure, buffeted by authority. His clothes were always a little too big for him and he shuffled rather than walked. His careworn, deeply lined face contrasted with a twinkle in his eyes, reflecting a whimsical sense of humour and a spirit which was rarely curbed. No man derived more pleasure from the simple act of leaning on a spade. With one foot resting on the blade and arms folded over the handle, he would address a stream of comical remarks to Tom Cosgrove and me as we worked. We protected him as best we could from being caught standing idle by the foreman. This did not happen very often, not because he was never idle but because he watched for the boss. The banter was endless between this little man who joked and shirked and the burly Cosgrove, who tolerantly did his own 'fair whack' and a bit more.

We had a trick for punctuating Billy's comments which rarely failed. One of us would look sharply over his shoulder and mutter 'look out'. To be caught unaware by the foreman was sacrilegious to him and he seemed to have a sixth sense when authority was nearby, but he could never be sure whether we had raised a false alarm, so the flow of chatter would stop as he worked his spade feverishly before furtively glancing round. If no one was there we had to endure a stream of oaths as we laughed, then he would resume his stance and chatter. One day, after some false alarms, we muttered urgently to him when the foreman was really behind him. Instead of looking round, he snorted defiance, abusing the foreman, assuming we were pulling his leg. After the foreman had finished with him he was as crestfallen as we were convulsed.

During this happy summer we worked as unskilled labourers, digging the foundations for a new housing estate. Even on wet days our spirits were rarely dampened. It was understood that we would not work outside in heavy rain: if the sky clouded over and we felt a few spots of rain Billy would announce he was 'soaked to the bloody skin' and retire to a shed. If the rain increased I followed, to be joined later by Tom Cosgrove, who always brought a set of draughts for this contingency. Billy would smoke a Woodbine and watch this highly intellectual game in respectful silence.

One Friday I asked the foreman if there was any weekend overtime as I needed the money. He told me of a reception to be held the following day at which Councillors were to watch a special film, in a municipal building with a glass roof. I was to pull tarpaulins over the roof just before the film and remove them afterwards. While I waited for the civic party to assemble, the leader of the Council, who was a friend, came over and urged me to join them. When I told him about the tarpaulins, he said: 'Pull the damn things over now and let this lot talk with the lights on'. I did so and joined the party. This incident was to affect the course of my life for the next fourteen years.

At the reception James McColl, the MP for Widnes, was one of the people who asked about my future plans. He recalled an advertisement he had seen for a producer's job in the BBC where one of the qualifications was some experience of the USA. I had only been there on my debating tour but the job seemed worth considering and McColl promised to send me the advertisement; it arrived three days after the closing date for applications. I telephoned Kenneth Adam, the Controller of the Light Programme in the BBC, whom I had met at Cambridge, and asked him how rigidly the Corporation adhered to these dates. He advised me to apply at once, explaining the delay and apologising for it. I sent off the letter and received a formal acknowledgement.

In the meantime I was invited to see Tom Williamson at the London office of the National Union of General and Municipal Workers. I had heard of him as one of the mighty trade union bosses who thundered at the TUC conference, so I expected to meet a fire-eater, but to my surprise he was a quiet, friendly man. He could be tough when necessary but he was pleasant to me and offered a job in the research department. The pay was poor, and he admitted this, but there was little he could do about it. It was September 1951 and after five years at college and three months labouring I felt it was time to make more constructive use of my qualifications.

The job marked the end of my old life in Widnes. Up till then Widnes had been my home, where I lived among family and friends; college had been a place to go for a term at a time. Whenever I returned home during my university years I picked up my old interests and sometimes started new campaigns. Now it was all over and, although I looked forward to the new job, I left my birthplace with many regrets.

In London I took temporary digs in a drab bedsitter in Belsize Park and went to work in the union office. I had to prepare information on such diverse subjects as gas, water, rubber and chemicals, and although much of the work was new to me I found it intensely interesting. The head of the department was Colin Chivers, a small, gay man who possessed an encyclopaedic knowledge of these industries. He gave me a warm welcome and I quickly settled down.

As Pauline and I were planning to be married at the end of the year, I became increasingly worried about money, because of the low pay for my work. I had almost forgotten about my application for a job as producer in the BBC's North American service, when quite unexpectedly I was asked to go for an interview. It reminded me of the scholarship boards; everyone was friendly and apparently casual. An obvious question, which I should have anticipated, caught me slightly off balance; I was asked to imagine producing a radio programme at short notice about an unfamiliar town—how would I go about it? I had no idea until I suddenly visualised Widnes—then I talked about all the interesting contacts I could think of, including civic leaders, employers, trade unionists, landlords, slum dwellers, local journalists and other characters. My blunderbuss approach would have produced a programme lacking in direction but so comprehensive that it must have included some good material. Eventually I was offered the job. Perhaps my debating tour of the USA influenced their decision since I had no production experience and my interest in radio was confined to news and music.

Before I was due to start work the 1951 General Election was announced. I wanted to fight it although the signs were not promising for the Labour Government. It had lived precariously since its majority had been slashed to six in the 1950 election. The vast post-war problems of the previous six years and the additional pressure of its miniscule majority had taken their toll; it was a tired and un-popular Government. I had no idea how to get nominated and as telephone calls to Transport House drew little response I telephoned Hugh Dalton, with whom I had debated at Cambridge. I knew he was a busy man as Minister of Local Government and Planning, but he had asked whether I was interested in a political career and suggested contacting him if I decided to try. It was perhaps taking him too much at his word, but he seemed pleased. 'So you want to have a go, eh?' he said, and the question seemed to express his satisfaction, though he could not promise anything. During the next week I received three or four letters from constituency Labour parties who had not yet nominated a candidate, asking if I was interested in applying.

Dalton had worked quickly and I was grateful. They were offers of political apprenticeships rather than passports to Parliament because in every case the Conservative majority was unassailable. Before I had replied to any of them I heard from Percy Clarke, a member of the Finchley Labour Party, who worked at Transport House. He told me that Finchley would shortly be selecting their candidate and I could be nominated for the selection conference. It was a safe Conservative seat, held by Sir John Crowder with a majority of over 12,000, but this was not as astronomical as some of the others, and I accepted with alacrity.

Within a week I attended my first selection meeting together with three other hopeful candidates. We huddled in a small room and each went in turn to address the conference. While we were together we confined ourselves to small talk to avoid revealing any political gems to opponents; political principles and rhetoric were saved for the conference itself. When my turn came I sat on the platform as the chairman read out my credentials to a mainly middle-class group of about a hundred people. He talked about my activities in Widnes and gave an impressive gloss to my academic qualifications from Oxford and Cambridge.

After my speech I answered questions, then left to rejoin the other candidates in the ante-room. Tension mounted until the final speaker finished and we all strained to hear the counting of votes. Suddenly one candidate leaned over to me and whispered that he thought I had got it—but he could not be sure.

The finale was theatrically staged. We were led to the platform to sit facing the delegates while the chairman explained how difficult the choice had been and so on. Finally he turned to me and said that I had been selected—whereupon I made a short speech of thanks. Aware of the other candidates' disappointment, I tried to disguise my delight at reaching the first stepping-stone to a Parliamentary career. But there was little time for self-congratulation. Polling day was less than a month away and we immediately had to prepare an election address and organise a series of tours and meetings throughout the constituency. It was different from my Council election; I had the support of a political machine but I knew I would not top the poll this time.

The basic issues had not changed much since the 1950 General Election. Full employment, fair shares, prices and nationalisation were to dominate the campaign, and controversies about Persia and Egypt also played a prominent part. Some people expected the Labour Party to lose, but the Government had a fine record, especially in view of the immense post-war difficulties. Full employment had been maintained and over a million houses had been built as part of a massive reconstruction project. Prices had inevitably risen but the cost of living compared favourably with that of our foreign competitors—though this did not impress some people. It was difficult to present price controls and food subsidies as an attractive electoral package. I spoke on these subjects all over the constituency and the meetings were well attended although my speeches were not always well received. One outraged listener wrote anonymously to tell me that it was the first time he had heard anyone from his alma mater, Cambridge, speak like an orang-utang. The criticism did not disturb me—only the fact that I could not reply.

Although victory was almost impossible I fought an energetic campaign with strong support from Party members. No one worked harder than an ardent Jewish socialist named Nat Birch, who was the Party's fund raiser. He attended every meeting, cajoling the audience with a fine mixture of special pleading and general flattery. If he knew someone was going to give a cheque he would ask him to delay handing it up to the platform until the psychological moment had arrived to start a flow of contributions. I always felt that Nat had just walked out of the bazaars of the Middle East; subtle, warm and kind, he added colour and gaiety to the campaign.

I was lent an old car, covered in 'Vote for Ashley' posters and carrying a huge loudspeaker. It seemed more suitable for a carnival than an election, especially as it made a loud thumping noise like a drum when I drove it. I took it to Cambridge when I visited Pauline, and the girls at Girton College probably thought she was marrying a wild exhibitionist. They enjoyed the fun and so did we, but we were puzzled about the big drum; it turned out to be the big end, which practically fell out on polling day.

Self-delusion is a political hazard, especially during elections. At the start of the campaign I knew there was no hope but by the end I began to wonder. Party officials assured me that I would get the support of most residents in the new housing estates and I allowed myself the luxury of thinking that we might pull off a surprise. It was a slight case of schizophrenia; basic political realities could not be altered by wishful thinking—but that did not prevent me from indulging in it a little until polling day. We made few converts from the Conservatives who won 200 more votes than in 1950. The Liberals lost 2,500, but I increased the Labour vote by nearly 1,000—a fair result considering the prevailing political mood. All over the country there had been a small, remarkably uniform swing to the Conservatives, and they took office with a narrow but decisive majority of seventeen. It was deeply disappointing and the prospect of another Conservative government was depressing. But it did not affect my political zeal.

Although I was due to start work at the BBC shortly after the election, I was still anxious to enter Parliament. This first Parliamentary election experience was a crossroads in my career. I discussed with Len Williams, the National Agent of the Labour Party, the possibility of getting another constituency. He said there were hundreds of bright young men seeking seats; I would be wiser to start work and acquire some kind of proficiency first, then consider Parliament later. His intentions were good and I took his advice, particularly as I was shortly to be married; but I have often wondered what might have happened had I rejected his advice. It was not without irony that the man I replaced in the BBC was Tony Wedgwood Benn, who had resigned to become the MP for Bristol, South East—and subsequently a Cabinet Minister.

9

BBC Radio Producer

In November 1951, I began work for the BBC in a large, cavernous building, formerly a hotel, opposite Broadcasting House. The North American section, which I joined, was part of the General Overseas Service but its producers had little association with others in the Service. A tightly knit, though cosmopolitan, group, they included a bearded, emotional Englishman who could produce splendid dramas and silly tantrums; a casual Canadian, able and unruffled; and an unbelievably loquacious Australian woman. They were led with patience and charm by an attractive Canadian named Rooney Pelletier.

Although he was head of the section he broadcast himself; his rich, deep voice seemed made for radio. My first job was to produce his weekly review of people and events in Britain. It must have been the easiest job in the BBC. Every Monday he would present me with the script of a ten-minute talk which I had to check and suggest improvements. Of course I could hardly improve the skilful script, though with deference to our professional relationship, that of contributor and producer, he accepted all but my most naive suggestions. Despite being head of the service and an experienced broadcaster, he scrupulously observed the rule that the responsibility for a programme lay with the producer. This was his diplomatic way of initiating me into my job. He was teaching me while I produced him, but he was too kind and tactful to show it.

I also produced a weekly four-minute talk on housewives' problems given by a pleasant woman named Rose Buckner. It was an equally simple job; Mrs Buckner had been broadcasting for many years and she needed no guidance from a producer; but I escorted her to the studio, suggested one or two minor changes in the script and carefully timed it to three minutes fifty seconds. Such were my early days in the BBC.

Most programmes expressed British opinion, but the impressions of visiting American tourists were of interest to their townsfolk at home. In the summer I went with a radio journalist, Stephen Grenfell, to Buckingham Palace, the Tower of London and Windsor

Castle where we recorded scores of tourist interviews which were transmitted to their local stations. Grenfell, a skilled reporter, must have found the work depressing because the questions had to be repetitive and the replies were predictable. The Americans were generous with their praise; they thought the Palace was terrific, the Tower historic and Windsor great. I wondered if they were bored, too, at the banal questions, but they rarely objected. The only enjoyable part of these visits was the drink with Grenfell afterwards; he was a tough, rumbustious character—a wit who recounted irreverent anecdotes about famous or pompous personalities.

The programmes were harmless and the BBC was easy-going unless anyone transgressed the unwritten code of conduct. In a series about the monarchy, a Canadian woman, who had a transatlantic attitude to 'Queen Liz', wrote an amusing and breezy script. When I objected to some parts of it she was surprised and invited me to her home where we had a lively discussion, her husband being particularly indignant that the BBC should censor the views of his wife. I agreed to the script with only a few changes but I took the precaution of referring it to the head of my department.

Rooney Pelletier had been replaced by a new head, who was astounded that I had not condemned such blasphemy. After all, we were not talking about tourists' impressions or housewives' chores but the monarchy. I had obviously failed to appreciate the titanic importance of the subject and ought to have rejected everything but the most serious and respectful account. The script was referred to the Service Controller who, I was told, unhesitatingly decided that it was unsuitable and I had made a serious error of judgement. There was some ruminative head-shaking at this; no doubt in the club and corridors colleagues murmured that the new man was not up to it. I found it all depressing, especially as I felt I was achieving nothing constructive with my work.

In response to my request for more creative programmes I was invited to produce a documentary about St Bride's Church, Fleet Street. It was hardly a breathtaking subject and I could not visualise the Americans rushing to their radios to hear the programme, but I felt I had to accept. The vicar co-operated, speaking eloquently of the history and activities of his church. Did I know of the crypt? He ordered the caretaker to show me the depths—and he was taken literally. In a grisly tour I was shown human remains stacked in boxes being rearranged by the caretaker, who gave me a sepulchral commentary on his work. Perhaps the dismal atmosphere affected me but my programme had a cool reception from the departmental head. Later, a more experienced producer was asked to 'tart it up a bit'. He added mournful music and echoing footsteps in the crypt which were supposed to create atmosphere. It all pleased the head but depressed me; apparently radio production was not the natural outlet for whatever talents I might possess. I wondered if it was time to seek a job elsewhere.

Near the end of 1951 I was much less interested in BBC programmes than in my forthcoming marriage. We hoped to marry in December but Pauline's mother wanted her to wait for eighteen months until she had got her degree. There had been a few married women undergraduates just after the war but generally girls were sent down if they married. I, too, was anxious that she should not sacrifice her university education and I went to see the Mistress of Girton, who agreed, after some discussion, that Pauline should be allowed to remain there after our marriage. The decision was important to us and also meant that future girl students no longer had to choose between marriage and a degree.

We did not have many friends in London at that time and most of the guests at our wedding, apart from family, were people we had known in Cambridge or the BBC. After the reception we drove with my sister Margaret to Widnes for another reception, this time with my family and local friends. We were very happy, although we spent the first night of our honeymoon in one of the most unromantic settings in the world—34 Wellington Street. Next day we went to the other extreme and travelled to the serene beauty of the Lake District.

The next eighteen months were difficult. Pauline and I were apart for much of the time while she was studying at Cambridge and I was working at the BBC in a job I disliked. I was not interested in tourist interviews and housewives' chats—still less skeletons—and inevitably my relations with the new head of the department deteriorated. He was unenthusiastic about my work, while I blamed him for insisting on fatuous programmes.

We had regular rows about trivial issues—and a major one when I applied for a pay increase. My request astonished him and I was summoned to his office where he sat behind a large desk, a small, grey man taking his responsibilities very seriously; it was clear that I had incurred his displeasure—again. He did not invite me to sit

down but sternly asked how I justified the application. Did I not realise that salaries were professionally assessed and carefully reviewed by the BBC's administrative department? I justified my claim vigorously, if a little imaginatively and perhaps extravagantly; no one who heard the simple programmes I produced would credit the vast amount of thought and effort that went into them. He was unimpressed and when I finished he replied, a little wearily and defensively, 'You know, Jack, I rather like you, but you make it difficult for me.' My application was rejected but I persisted in pestering him. At length it was granted, but it took so long that I was probably due for a rise in any case.

Soon afterwards Pauline left Cambridge. She held a college scholarship in mathematics but after her first year changed to economics—to the dismay of her mathematics tutor; although she spent only two years reading economics she got an upper second in her final degree. After discussing matters with her, I decided to leave the BBC as I was so unhappy there and I applied for a job as a personnel officer at Philips Electrical Company. I explained that I would like to discuss the job but was not certain I wanted it—a frank approach which was not warmly welcomed. However, they were interested because of my record and after a series of interviews I was offered the job. But I had meant what I said at the first interview. I wanted to think about it because I was not sure how far I would be allowed to conciliate and how much I would be expected, in the last resort, to oppose the trade unions: that would be out of the question for me.

The man who had held the job previously, Peter Parker, was known to friends of mine and they arranged for me to meet him. At the end of our talk, after casually mentioning that he had spent a year on a fellowship in the United States, he suggested that as Pauline and I were unsettled we might like to consider going abroad. A few days later I sought information at the American Embassy: most of the available scholarships and fellowships for that year had already been taken, but I was just in time to apply for one of the highly prized Commonwealth Fund Fellowships. These provided a year in the United States, studying any subject of one's choice; I selected the relationship between American broadcasting and politics.

I was interviewed by a distinguished body of University Vice-Chancellors who asked me about my proposed plans for studying in America. Eventually the chairman looked round the table, inviting any further questions. One benign, rather elderly member shook his head, saying that he had attended one of my debates in the United States and, in effect, so far as he was concerned I should get the fellowship; he was Sir James Duff, the Vice-Chancellor of Durham University, and I appreciated his intervention. I was awarded the fellowship, but I deferred my visit to the United States because Pauline was expecting our first baby. We decided to wait until the baby was three months old, when I would go alone and Pauline would follow in a further three months.

A few days later I was invited to join Stephen Bonarjee, head of the current affairs unit in the BBC's Home Service. Although I would only be available for six months before going to the United States he was not deterred. The main obstacle was the attitude of the Controller of the Home Service, Mary Somerville, who was initially opposed to my transfer because I had been a political candidate—but she overcame her misgivings and I began one of my happiest periods in broadcasting.

BBC radio was then much more important than it is today. It still had large evening audiences for news and current affairs programmes which enjoyed enormous prestige. Authority and reliability, established before the war and enhanced during it, were conspicuous in Broadcasting House when I moved in. Although it shared the same values as the overseas services it seemed a different world, one in which the traditional attitudes of the BBC were paramount. Producers were well-informed, well-spoken and well-behaved—middle-class products with Eton and Harrow well represented. Their discussions were decorous, language restrained and they would sooner drop their salary than drop an 'h'.

I thought it was a breeding ground for conformity and complacency—but I was wrong. Beneath this placid exterior each man—or woman—felt deeply about the values of public service broadcasting in general, and the standards of their own programmes in particular. They were professionals, jealous of their traditions, proud of their products.

The programmes, 'At Home and Abroad' and 'Topic for Tonight', dealt mainly with political and industrial matters. I found them absorbing, bringing me into close contact with leading politicians, trade unionists and industrialists. The interviewers were interesting people and some, like Campbell Fraser and Francis Williams, were to become close and lasting friends.

Major controversies of the day were reported and analysed; occasionally the BBC itself was the subject. When the Musicians' Union went on strike against the BBC about payment for the use of recordings, I was asked to produce an item with Hardie Ratcliffe, General Secretary of the Musicians' Union, and Sir Ian Jacob, Director-General of the BBC. My own socialist views and close links with the trade union movement were well known because I made no attempt to disguise them, but as a professional producer it was my job to ensure fair play. Steve Bonarjee, as head of the unit, was naturally involved in the early discussions about the programme, and he had dealt directly with the Director-General. On the night the programme was to be transmitted he suggested I should take Hardie Ratcliffe while he produced the Director-General. I was unwilling. He was probably being helpful, but I interpreted it as a personal criticism. The day was saved by Steve making a diplomatic and gracious withdrawal which I appreciated more in retrospect than I did at the time.

Sometimes we faced insoluble problems. I once arranged for Randolph Churchill to interview Aristotle Onassis about shipbuilding. It was a controversial subject at that time and Onassis had been in the headlines for days. He came with his lovely wife, Tina, and the ebullient Randolph Churchill who had obviously been celebrating something before he arrived. It was interesting to see Churchill dominating the powerful Onassis; his intimate references to 'Ary' evoked deferential responses from the tycoon. But Churchill was somewhat merry; when I was taking him to the fourth floor studio for a voice test, the lift stopped at the first floor; assuming we had arrived, he stepped out just as the automatic doors closed. I reached the studio floor without my interviewer and dashed down the stairs shouting 'Mr Churchill' on each floor. But there was no sign of him. Finally I went to the hospitality suite to report to Stephen Bonarjee, and there was an angry Churchill disputing the decision to drop the programme, while Onassis, looking a little relieved, sympathised. Tina Onassis stood quietly aloof. Churchill was angry, yet I found his flamboyant fight against the decision engaging and the more I saw of him later the more I liked him.

While producing these programmes I became aware of the distinctive spirit animating BBC producers. Within Broadcasting House natural differences of opinion sometimes led to heated discussions, even intrigue. Yet in their dealings with public men, politicians, industrialists, trade unionists and administrators, they acted as one. It was akin to the comradeship of the Services. If it had the vice of appearing to be smug, it had the virtue of confidence in colleagues, all motivated by the same zeal for public service broadcasting. Whatever the pressures, the BBC always fought for its principles and if it irked its foes it heartened its friends, particularly those of us who faced frequent pressures from all sides.

We learned to parry the thrusts and threats, the pressure and pleading, regardless of the source. Most demands were from politicians, many of whom were convinced that the other side was favoured—or so they said. Instead of giving them more time we showed them the record. Businessmen were less direct but equally forceful, wanting programmes 'about industry' although all too often they meant advertisements for their firms. But few if any were successful, since BBC rules about advertising were strict. The chairman of ICI might find himself referred to as the head of a large chemical company; people could guess, but he might equally have been the boss of Boots.

During my six months in Broadcasting House I learned not only about the BBC but about the broadcasters. And it was the politicians who revealed themselves most. They were astonishingly frank about their colleagues when they came to the studios; the more senior they were the more polished was their hatchet work. I would have been happy to stay in this fascinating job, but it was time to set off on my second journey to the USA.

10

Scholarship in the USA

I felt no sense of novelty when I arrived in New York for my second visit; the skyscrapers, neon lights and breathless pace all seemed familiar. The only new sensation was loneliness. I felt it nowhere more keenly than in the YMCA building where I went to stay; it seemed crowded, impersonal and alien to me.

As I went for a shower that evening a massive youth came and watched, silently smoking a cigarette. He followed me to my room and a few moments later there was a quiet knock at the door. The youth's eyes roved around my room as he asked me for a match. I went to get one, but a sixth sense warned me—as I suddenly wheeled round he was pushing his way in. We wrestled briefly until I forced him into the corridor and slammed the door. As I had come to America to study rather than to fight I moved next day to a hotel.

Officials at the headquarters of the Commonwealth Fellowship, who were helpful without imposing themselves, readily assisted in making any arrangements I wished but avoided foisting an itinerary on me. The senior official, E. K. Wickham, a small, rotund man with a nimble mind, had a ready grasp of the problems of visiting English students. His mature and friendly approach was a hallmark of the Fellowship. His assistant, a jovial raconteur named Lance Hammond, enjoyed life with gusto, showering goodwill like confetti. The third member of this well-balanced trio was a clear-eyed woman named Martha English, who did much of the organisational work. Together they formed a haven of friendship in the urban jungle of New York.

Soon after my arrival I contacted the BBC's New York office and later I visited the suburban home of Alec Sutherland, the American representative. A Scotsman who had happily settled in the United States, he amused me by his laconic though friendly attitude to his adopted country. 'You can see the West in the East,' he said as he took me to a hotel bar with cowboy décor where we drank neat whisky in the presumed style of old Western heroes. That was the first time I tried it; next morning, I vowed it would be the last. I stayed with him for a few days and before leaving I bought an Oldsmobile car from one of his friends, a garage proprietor. My first-ever car—it cost about 300 dollars, less than £100—was enough to spoil me for any other. It had a radio, automatic gear-change and electric push buttons for the windows and sliding roof. It was large even by American standards and massive compared with British cars. I felt like a millionaire as I surveyed this sleek monster which I was to drive across the United States. But first I needed a driving licence.

I planned to drive to Louisville, Kentucky, but I could not arrange a driving test until the day I was due to leave. In England applicants get their certificate as soon as they pass and I expected the same procedure in New York, but after my test the examiner said I would be informed in due course. His brusque manner persuaded me that I would jeopardise my chances by pressing for the result. My cases were packed in the car, I was reluctant to wait indefinitely, so without a licence I set off on the long drive to Kentucky. It was a tiring journey in an unfamiliar car across strange country and, instead of being stimulated, I felt low and lonely. I was relieved when I arrived in Louisville, where I stayed for the next six weeks.

At that time American towns like Louisville generally had about half a dozen small, competing radio and television stations. Some broadcast only music and local news though most of them supplemented their service with news and other programmes from the national networks. These stations, based on a small community, were in striking contrast to the BBC, then a monopoly, which gave all listeners the same limited choice between a few national programmes, plus a small number from the regions.

In Louisville the major radio and television stations were under the same ownership as the excellent local newspaper, the *Courier*. The chairman, Barry Bingham, a cultivated and knowledgeable Southerner, gave me complete freedom during my stay and all the staff were very friendly; the newsmen even invited me to chase the news with them. Their van was fitted with a police radio and they tried racing police to the scenes of crimes. This helped them to make excellent news programmes since they caught people's first reactions rather than their second thoughts: a man who has just been robbed speaks with more feeling when he has not had time to reflect that the insurance company will pay.

After some weeks in Louisville, I planned further trips to radio and television stations in Tennessee and Florida. I was anxious to make use of my opportunity to travel and found the Southerners unbelievably generous in their hospitality to someone they had never met; one person would recommend a visit to another, creating a chain of friendship which was invaluable to me as a lone student ranger. In Nashville, Tennessee, I stayed with a professor, a friendly man with a great regard for Britain. When I mentioned that I intended to go to Georgia he simply picked up the telephone and rang to another professor, who invited me to stay.

In Georgia I nearly came to an untimely end when I went alone on a fishing trip on a huge lake. After I had fished for a while, I went swimming, although I am a poor swimmer. I waded and floated in the water for some time until I suddenly found that I was well out of my depth. I struck out for the shore but when I had nearly exhausted myself it seemed as far away as ever; I was still in deep water so I put my head down and flailed away weakly. At the extreme limit of endurance, I sank, and to my unbelievable relief my feet touched the bottom. I lay exhausted and vomiting in the shallow water; instead of the idyllic lake I had seen on arrival, it had nearly been a death trap. I was lucky.

For the next few months I toured broadcasting stations, gradually working my way back to New York to meet Pauline and the baby. I was particularly interested in the influence of sponsors on television standards, but it was difficult to assess. Each network insisted that there was no sponsor control over their news programmes—but then each of them claimed it had the best shows and largest audiences. They were sometimes accused of committing sins of omission at the behest of sponsors—particularly when one television news programme sponsored by a tobacco firm failed to mention an important report on the connection between smoking and lung cancer. When I asked one of the programme's producers if it was true that the sponsor had insisted on deleting the item, he said the cigarette–cancer relationship had been mentioned many times since. This evasive answer was disturbing, the more so when he added that he 'wouldn't lean over backwards to offend a sponsor'.

Yet the Americans, despite the pressures of commercialism and sponsorship, were slowly creating television standards crucial to a democratic society. Whatever the faults of their programmes, the producers, especially those working in the networks, fought to establish important principles. One was that no matter how exalted the interviewee he was not allowed to dictate the questions to be asked. Some sacrifices were made to defend this principle: during the United Nations anniversary celebrations, Mr Molotov accepted an invitation to appear in a network interview. I saw how delighted the producers were with this scoop, especially as network competition was intense. Then Molotov sent in a list of questions he was prepared to answer. The network cancelled the show and lost their scoop rather than accept this restriction on their freedom.

I was delighted to meet Pauline and six-months-old Jacqueline in New York. After my tour of the Southern states I was struck by Pauline's English accent; she was shocked by American prices. We stayed briefly at a small hotel, and when we needed a quarter pint of warmed milk for the baby's cereal it cost half a dollar. Pauline immediately went out and bought a small portable cooker which was useful for preparing the baby's food and making tea for us.

During the next six months we travelled from coast to coast, improvising as we went; on average we stayed in two different bedrooms each week. I wanted to visit as many radio and television stations as possible but it would have been wiser to have stayed at the three main broadcasting network centres, New York, Chicago and Hollywood. As it was, the car became baby's home. Luckily it was large enough to carry her equipment which included a carry cot, an English pram and an American pushchair—complete with sunshade. She soon became accustomed to the rhythmic tempo of the car and cried when it stopped. Traffic lights in towns were a particular nuisance but I learned to slow the car, glide towards the lights and gradually accelerate as they changed. We also developed a technique for cooking the baby's food in the car. At first we stopped to heat tins in a pan of water on our small stove but as we drove through humid heat without any air conditioning we simply placed a tin just behind the windscreen; it was heated as effectively as on the stove.

On these car journeys I learnt more about American radio programmes than when I visited the studios. Some of the programmes were awful, especially those from the 'music, news and sports' stations. There was plenty of music but its quality did not match its quantity. 'Good' music was not provided as generously as by the BBC; garrulous disc jockeys introduced pop records with a string of superlatives matched only by stupendous descriptions of the soap and cornflakes which they sold. The output of these stations was defended by one local manager who said 'I give 'em lots of music because drama takes too much thought and concentration. People don't want that—if they do, they get it on television.' He was talking of soap operas. There were over 1,400 of these disc-jockey stations scattered throughout the States and they all made a profit.

Local radio was novel to me; nothing comparable with it existed in Britain. In America one of the main attractions of local radio in small communities was the friendly and intimate nature of the news which, in very small places, sometimes sounded like gossip. I heard local news bulletins with such items as 'Mr and Mrs Hiram K. Smith had four friends to dinner last night and they played bridge until midnight... Mr and Mrs Ed Jones returned early today from their holiday in Florida where they stayed with their daughter Jane, who settled there ten years ago when she married...' This news made visitors smile but the stations were taking advantage of local radio's greatest asset—its ability to personalise local events which were of intimate concern to its listeners.

Our first stay in an American community was, curiously enough, with an English family from Widnes. They were Harry and Gwen Anderson, who not only came from Widnes but had actually worked in the factory where I was a shop steward. Gwen was an attractive young red-haired girl who had driven the trucks I used to borrow at lunch time to career around the factory. Her husband, a Rugby League footballer, had played for Widnes and made a great reputation. Not long after their marriage they emigrated and settled near Boston. We had an enjoyable time with them, talking about old friends and discussing mutual impressions of the United States. It was 1955 and we were impressed by the motorways and supermarkets which were unfamiliar to us. They were to become commonplace in Britain in the following decade but at that time they were an exciting novelty and Harry and Gwen enjoyed introducing us to them.

The Andersons' standard of living was much higher than it had been in England. But during the tour we were invited to stay with some prosperous American families who had luxurious homes full of gadgetry. In Denver, Colorado, we were guests of a brain surgeon and his wife who met us at the English Speaking Union. Their large, beautiful house was equipped with a kitchen which impressed Pauline, who had coped magnificently with domestic chores on our journey. It had an automatic washer, cooker, fridge, freezer, drier and disposal unit, and there was even a maid to press the switches. It was a striking example of American affluence.

We toured the country against an ever-changing backcloth of rolling prairies and arid deserts—yet the townships, cars, clothes and food remained much the same. And nothing was more uniform than the broadcasts. Radio and television stations produced the same curious mixture of the brilliant and the banal. Local stations in small communities were unpretentious but popular, while large ones in big cities were affluent and impersonal. In Hollywood the glitter and glamour of film studios were finally fading before the power of television.

Before turning eastward we visited some American friends in Berkeley, California. Jeffrey Cohelan and his family had been friends of ours in England when he was studying British trade unions. A placid but articulate trade union official, he had political ambition and later became a Congressman. With him and his wife, Evelyn, and their four children we had a happy few weeks, resting from the tour. A few days after we joined them they were due to move house and most people would have diplomatically suggested it was time for their visitors to leave; in fact we suggested it but they turned the idea down flatly. So we all went together in a gay, confused removal. Jeffrey insisted that I must speak to his trade union colleagues, tour the university, meet local politicians and, of course, visit the radio and television stations. He usually explained to the people we met—with a twinkle in his eye—that I was an expert in their subject in England. No matter how I tried to disabuse them I was expected to speak authoritatively about British trade unions, Oxford and Cambridge, and the BBC.

After our enjoyable stay with the Cohelans, we left with great reluctance, but it was time to begin the eastward return journey. On the long drive to New York, a dreary contrast to our stay in Berkeley, we had a slight brush with the law. As we drove along a sun-baked road, Pauline wearing a bikini, Jacqueline a nappy and myself a pair of shorts, we were flagged down by an armed policeman on a motor cycle. He claimed we had crossed a double yellow line some miles back; under arrest, we were to be escorted back to town. We had not been pulled up earlier because he had been chasing somebody else. When I asked him to lead the way back he grinned and ordered me to go ahead of him.

Feeling rather silly being escorted practically at gun point for a traffic offence, we were taken to a large, secluded house on the outskirts of a small town. The judge invited us into his living room while a formal charge was written out by the policeman. While this was going on the judge played with Jacqueline on his knee; then assuming a stern expression he handed her over to Pauline, read the charge sheet, and asked me if I had anything to say. Clad only in a pair of shorts, I didn't know whether to remain seated on his settee or stand respectfully, but I rose and asked him if he would consider a plea in mitigation. He did not seem familiar with the phrase but invited me to say anything I wanted, so I embarked on a comparative assessment of the British and American road regulations and the difficulties of visitors who were strangers to the American system. When I had finished the judge said I would have to pay a fine but he would 'knock off the costs' which, he explained, meant that his town got nothing out of the business.

We headed for Washington where I wanted to see the Congressional radio and television operation in the Capitol. Politicians had quickly recognised the growing power of television, and Senators and Congressmen had their own television studio in the Capitol. It was a simple affair in the basement; the only 'props' behind a desk and chair were bookcases with imitation book backs and a picture of the Capitol behind a glassless window frame. But it was highly efficient. As most Congressmen were unpunctual, schedules meant little, and the atmosphere was relaxed and informal. I met and chatted with many American leaders, including such people as Vice-President Nixon, Postmaster Summerfield, and a host of Senators who were awaiting their turn before the camera.

Some of the Senators I watched delivering straight talks to camera tried to be objective, and a few succeeded. Others were heavily partisan with an obvious view to the next election. Probably through long experience, many of them were surprisingly effective with apparently little or no production. The interviews were done with a slickness and style that the best of professionals would admire but the smoothness masked the relative superficiality of the questioning. Each Senator was fed the kind of questions all politicians pray for when they are performing before the multitude.

Interviews between Congressmen and high-ranking leaders lacked sparkle. They were, no doubt, designed to be cosy. For example, Vice-President Nixon was interviewed by Republican Congressmen while I was there, and the scene was strongly reminiscent of meetings between candidates and famous party officials in a candidate's home town. 'Well, Mr Vice-President, the folks I represent are proud to have you come and talk to them . . .' 'Well, Jim, I only hope your folks know what a splendid job you are doing for them here in Washington.'

Politicians were naturally anxious to use television but their activities disturbed some people. Could a politician justify appearing as narrator, or acting as guide on a filmed tour of Washington for a film he had never seen? One outstanding politician I saw tried five times to complete the script as guide to a tour. He failed because he did not want to wear his spectacles before the camera and yet without them he could not read an unfamiliar script on the teleprompter. But the most serious criticism was reserved for the 'ghost' interview. From a script of questions and answers a Cabinet member or high-ranking official recorded a film of the answers only; days or weeks later any Congressman could walk into the studio and ask the scripted questions—and then the Cabinet member's filmed answers were dubbed in.

By the time I left Washington to return to the BBC I was deeply interested in the growing influence of television on politics. It was revealing, under its microscopic lens, men who had previously been merely names or reputations, mirroring the image which they chose to put on public display. But would the mirror distort? And could the image be faked? No ready answers were available, but these questions were important. The relationship was inevitably reciprocal and it was fascinating to see not only how the medium used politicians but how politicians used the medium.

11

BBC Television Producer

In 1957 BBC television was fighting a desperate battle for its future —and apparently losing. Deprived of its monopoly two years earlier, it was now losing its audience. Commercial television claimed a 79:21 preference over BBC and many broadcasters were wondering where the slide would end; already some people were reluctant to pay a licence fee. As the BBC's audience fell, the volume of complaints rose proportionately. 'Why,' viewers asked, 'should we pay for a service we never watch?' Many BBC producers still clung to the Reithian philosophy that the BBC's duty was to produce high-quality programmes irrespective of popular appeal; they felt that any attempt to seek a mass audience would inevitably mean abandoning cherished standards. But young men were challenging the old. New creative talents were fighting their battle on two fronts—against commercial television and against some of their own colleagues.

Soon after my return from America I was invited to become a television producer, specialising in industrial affairs. On my arrival at Lime Grove I was given a tepid reception by some of the impatient younger producers who probably suspected that I was tainted with the old traditions after working in Broadcasting House. My status, as a producer rather than a trainee, must have created resentment since I had no experience of television. But I had been invited because there were no producers with first-hand experience of industry on the shop floor.

Complaints had been made, with good reason, about the poor coverage of industrial affairs on television and I was expected to remedy this. The question for me was how to do so, because in the so-called 'Talks Department', as then constituted, there was an assortment of programmes including wide-ranging magazines and single-subject documentaries. Programmes competed and producers conflicted.

There were several clearly defined groups in television Talks Department at that time, though none was formally organised. The liveliest consisted of bright young men, thrustful and eager to break new ground in blitzkrieg style. Talented and aggressive, they referred to the quieter, older people as men with bomber-pilot attitudes compared with their own fighter-pilot approach.

Two of the most dynamic young producers were Donald Baverstock and Michael Peacock. Baverstock was an innovator; his programme *Tonight*, based on the earlier *Highlight*, made a decisive breakthrough in the previously more formal programme presentation. The equivalent of a popular daily newspaper, it consisted of short, colourful items varying in pace and depth. Although this format is familiar today, it was then new and startling with its harassing type of interviews and irreverent, sceptical approach. Peacock edited the heavier, though equally professional, *Panorama*, a weekly current affairs programme which took itself more seriously with its 'in depth' analysis of major issues.

The older men were no less able, although they generally had quieter and more reflective dispositions. While the so-called fighter-pilot producers bubbled and effervesced, exploiting controversial issues and personalities, the bomber-pilot group eschewed what they called 'argy-bargy shows' and preferred thoughtful and constructive, if less exciting, programmes.

The younger men were deservedly praised for their new style, which was to become the dominant one in the years ahead. They were the fashionable favourites of BBC executives, but I felt that their arrogance could have been slightly toned down without affecting their basic drive, and the older men, who were by no means old, could have been encouraged to exercise their less volatile but clearly valuable talents.

A third group was composed of men like Huw Wheldon and David Attenborough, who were outstanding producers; in some ways they were above the battle, unchallenged because of their great professional expertise. Wheldon had a shining and provocative intelligence, though he never used one word if a dozen would do. Attenborough, at home before and behind the camera, is one of the very few men in television (or anywhere else) who seem to attract the undiluted affection of everyone who comes into contact with him. These two men were later to control the destiny of BBC television, Wheldon as the Managing Director and Attenborough as Controller of Programmes; neither lost his charm in the process, though they are as formidable a pair as could be found at the head of any British enterprise.

The best performances of all, never shown on the screen, were at the departmental meetings held every Thursday morning at Lime Grove. Into these post-mortems on the past week's programmes were tossed wit, banalities, epigrams, scorn, praise and sheer bloody-mindedness. The unenviable task of controlling these meetings, and organising the work of this turbulent department, fell to a rather diffident man, Leonard Miall. He had a high reputation as a journalist, having served for some time as the BBC's American correspondent, but he never seemed completely at ease in his administrative role as head of the department.

The personality who bestrode this stage majestically, if un-crowned, was the Assistant Head, Grace Wyndham Goldie, an intense, birdlike woman passionately absorbed in television. Producers divided their time between producing programmes and discussing the latest opinions or exploits of Mrs Goldie. Some people regarded her as queen of the jungle, strong and cunning, with respect for those who could hold their own and little patience for the weak and vulnerable. She was certainly a very impatient executive with no inhibitions about exercising her authority, but if at times it included some hectoring of harassed producers, it was all devoted to the cause of better television. I noticed that she always showed personal consideration to those she professionally attacked, trying to find some suitable role for them elsewhere if she felt they were inadequate. Proud of her successful protegés, she showed an emotional, almost maternal, concern for all her lively brood.

Mrs Goldie constantly pressed her producers to improve television standards and achieve better programmes. Greater imagination was needed, new ideas must be produced, more energy was required, costs should be cut and magnificent programmes should be the rule rather than the exception. Of course it was impossible to keep up with her ambitious ideas but they were never less than stimulating and often inspiring. Exceptionally knowledgeable, she was one of the most creative thinkers in television, and she made a significant contribution to the BBC's quality.

Soon after I arrived in television I was invited to work on *Panorama*, the weekly current affairs programme which described itself as a window on the world. At that time it was the most important and influential programme on television, with a regular audience of up to ten million. Apart from occasional amusing items, it analysed major controversies at home and abroad with a mixture of film reports, live outside broadcasts and studio inserts. It was the pride of BBC television.

Each Tuesday the production team met to review the previous night's programme, discuss ideas for the next one and provisionally plan a filming schedule. Developments during the week could make nonsense of the most careful plans, and often did so, but we could not sit around all week waiting for last-minute dramas. These could be dealt with live in the studio, so the main purpose of our early meeting was to plan the week's filming. For major items there might be general discussion about the best method of production, but generally the details were left to the person assigned to the story.

Most producers preferred to have a few days to organise their contributors and plan locations before filming in the latter part of the week. It was a sensible approach for a programme transmitted on Monday night. But as we had a camera crew always available, the editor naturally wanted them used at the beginning of the week to avoid overwork and congestion later. I ambitiously attempted to film some stories by going straight out on location with a reporter and camera crew and although this helped the general administrative planning of *Panorama*, it did not help me—it also led to strained relationships between some reporters and myself. Their exasperation was understandable since I sometimes directed the filming while sitting at a telephone making arrangements for the next location.

The relationship between a producer and a programme performer is subtle and complicated. A producer, usually a BBC staff man, has the final responsibility of translating an idea into a programme— deciding its shape and content, inviting participants and making studio and location arrangements for the camera crew. The commentator or interviewer, usually on short-term contract, takes no part in handling the general organisation and administrative arrangements. Naturally he is as concerned as the producer to make the best programme possible but sometimes there are differences about the means of achieving it. When personal relationships were good, as they usually were, the difficulties could be resolved amicably, but without the lubricant of professional friendship the relationship could become quite difficult.

Occasionally television reporters attempted to influence production techniques. On *Panorama* I once produced a programme, with Woodrow Wyatt, about prostitution. We filmed interviews with some prostitutes, and then I planned one with a publican; he was to talk about the effects of new legislation on public houses frequented by prostitutes. On location I set up the cameras and lighting and waited for Woodrow to arrive. He turned up quite late after what had probably been a lengthy lunch.

With no apology, he told me that he intended to start by speaking straight to camera, then turn and begin the interview. I told him to start with the interview and do the introduction live in the studio. After we had argued about this at some length and he had apparently agreed, I directed the camera to begin; he immediately turned to it and started on the introductory piece. I stopped shooting at once. Woodrow then warned me that unless I agreed to his method he would go home, whereupon I handed him his overcoat. He is not a big man but I had to admire the way he swaggered out with an air of injured innocence, as if he had been gravely insulted. I had always liked him and admired his courage, but that day I was angry. My anger dissolved into laughter a few days later when a girl telephoned the duty officer to complain that she was a prostitute who had 'done a job' for Woodrow Wyatt but had not yet been paid for it. I hastily explained that the job she had done was an interview for the programme.

Although differences between a producer and 'anchor man' were sometimes inevitable, because each held strong views about what constituted a good programme, they would invariably unite if anyone else attempted to influence the content of its presentation. This happened whether the issue was large or small. When I was filming an item in a northern steel factory with Robert Kee, we invited one of the shop stewards to be interviewed. He was the Mayor of the town but I urged him to come for the interview dressed in working clothes, in his role as shop steward. His wife insisted that it would be undignified for the Mayor to appear before the camera in dirty overalls and he turned up in his Sunday best. Kee and I had a quick word together, then we filmed the interview with him dressed as he was, in front of the furnaces. I later wrote to explain that he would not be in the programme due to a technical problem. In fact, there was no film in the camera.

When I was transferred to television I hoped to deal with relationships between trade unions and employers and to convey something of the atmosphere in industry, so familiar to those working in it but unknown and misunderstood by others. Unfortunately when it was at its most interesting, as during any dramatic strike, both sides were reluctant to take part in a programme, and after a dispute neither side wished to rake the ashes. I wanted to produce a programme on the famous unofficial strike at the Acton car works of the Rootes Group in 1961, but my approaches to the firm's directors and the leaders of the Amalgamated Engineering Union were firmly rejected. When I tried to find the unofficial strike leaders the pickets were very suspicious but after a long delay and many telephone calls they agreed to drive me to a garage near the factory for a meeting. The leaders were cool and tough. They said they would take part in the proposed programme if I would accept some obviously pre-arranged outrageous demands for large fees to each member of the strike committee, and a guarantee that every word they uttered would be included in the programme.

I was in a better negotiating position than the employers as I stood to lose only a non-existent programme. Eventually the strike leaders withdrew their demands, accepting a reasonable fee and my assurance of fair representation in the programme. I returned to Bill Carron, the President of the AEU, and when I told him that his unofficial shop stewards were taking part in the programme he changed his mind and decided he had better co-operate. Armed with all my film I returned to the employers and this time it wasn't too difficult to persuade them to participate. It was an unusual way of winning the co-operation of three conflicting industrial groups but it worked; after receiving the usual veto I was able to present the intricacies and conflicts of a particularly bitter and protracted industrial dispute.

The shop stewards, like so many trade unionists, had been cautious, even suspicious, of television. They had not been playing hard to get; they felt genuinely hostile, expecting all kinds of tricks to be played on them. After accepting my assurances, they presented their case cogently and articulately. They were untypical. In other programmes I found that some trade unionists—if they overcame their suspicions and took part at all—would insist on reading a prepared statement, especially if they were on strike. Nothing could be duller or less convincing, yet it was difficult, and sometimes impossible, to persuade them to do anything else. It was years before a few eloquent shop stewards began to demonstrate that a trade unionist can be as persuasive as anyone else on television, but even then it was not widely accepted by the movement as a whole.

However at that time there were a few notable exceptions, the most outstanding being Les Cannon and Frank Chapple of the Electrical Trades Union, who played a major role in an unusual power struggle. A small group of men gained control of this union, the sixth largest in the country, with nearly a quarter of a million members whose work services most major industries. The one per cent of members who were Communists controlled the ninety-nine per cent who were non-Communist; they manipulated the union and maintained themselves in office by fraud until Cannon and Chapple exposed them. Some remarkable tricks were used to ensure the election of leaders, including the disqualification of inconvenient votes from over fifty towns. The Communists at the ETU Head Office produced envelopes displaying postmarks as evidence that the votes they contained had been posted too late. But the further away from London these envelopes were posted, the later the postmark. This suggested that someone might have driven from London northwards, posting fraudulent envelopes back to Head Office, which were then produced as evidence. To test this theory a private enquiry agent made a trip from London to Scotland, posting envelopes at the main ETU branch centres; the time stamps on all his envelopes were exactly the same as on those used by the Communists to justify disqualification. Few trade union leaders ever had such dramatic stories, or could speak as articulately, as these two men.

Cannon and I became close friends, perhaps because of our similar backgrounds. He was a working-class man from Wigan, near Widnes, and we often joked about each other's home town. An easy-going sense of humour contrasted with his hard and unrelenting attitude to his opponents. His bluntness did not endear him to his colleagues on the General Council of the Trades Union Congress, but his intelligence and personality soon made him one of the outstanding union leaders in Britain. Refreshingly free from cant, he was an impressive speaker although he scorned histrionics. By his early death from cancer, the British trade union movement lost one of the few men who could have fanned the wind of radical change.

Difficult as it was to convey industrial attitudes on television, I found that when I produced a series called 'Does class matter?' the problems of illustrating and disentangling class attitudes were even more complicated. The narrator was Christopher Mayhew, MP, public schoolboy and son of a knight; he had little in common with me, St Patrick's elementary schoolboy and son of a labourer. Although he was highly competent, our relationship was hardly harmonious, for our instinctive reactions to any situation were invariably different and sometimes diametrically opposed. Mayhew was patient, but he must have been sorely tried by my refusal to accept many of his ideas and my intention to conduct the programme in a different way from his.

Eventually we sank our differences and pooled our resources; Mayhew had many lively ideas and I had more experience of class differences than anyone in the BBC. He conducted a poll which showed that the five things determining social position, in order of importance, were education, accent, job, family background, and wealth, and we allocated a programme to each. Our series was complicated, yet it over-simplified, maybe because our attempt to televise such subtle differences was over-ambitious. All the visual devices, roving cameras, interviews, descriptive diagrams and statistics added little to the general understanding of subjective, almost mystical, attitudes.

One of the most outstanding contributions to the series was made by a brilliant young Oxford undergraduate who had been a miner. He was refreshingly frank with us and revealed his deep feelings about class problems when he spoke of the difficulties he found at home. Before the programme was broadcast, a Sunday newspaper correspondent expressed interest and asked if he could see the transcript. I agreed without hesitation. A few days afterwards the headline in this newspaper read: 'Miner's Son at Oxford Ashamed of Home. The Boy who Kept His Father Secret.' The story misinterpreted the student and misquoted me. I was deeply angered, so was Mayhew, and we sent a telegram to the student, Dennis Potter—later a distinguished playwright—dissociating ourselves from the report. It was all we could do, but it probably did nothing to ease the embarrassment he must have felt after he had successfully dealt with a subtle problem in a frank and mature way. The newspaper report underlined how difficult it was to portray the subtleties of British class relationships on television.

The BBC was right to try to use my experience of working-class life but in some programmes it was valueless. A new programme called *Monitor*, dealing with the arts, was introduced with Huw

Wheldon as compère. The programme controllers, afraid that it might be too highbrow, felt that my down-to-earth approach might be a counter-balance. I was appointed Associate Producer, despite my warning that I was no expert on painting, sculpture or the theatre, and knew little of the personalities in these fields.

For one programme I was asked to invite the playwright John Osborne to discuss the theatre; when I spoke to him on the telephone he seemed indifferent and uninterested. I did not want to beg, and his manner deterred me from trying to persuade, so I simply said, 'Right you are, then,' and rang off. I was asked to repeat this conversation to Huw Wheldon and the editor, and I did so. When I finished their eyes met and Wheldon muttered savagely, 'Well done, Jack.' He brushed aside my argument that Osborne did not want to appear anyhow with the comment that I had not appreciated how important the playwright was. He was, of course, quite right. No playwright was that important to me.

Throughout this period, the late fifties, television was constantly seeking new ways of presenting political issues. At least it tried to do so between elections, since until 1959 the BBC's only role in a general election had been to lend its transmitters for Party broadcasts. Once an election campaign began, the BBC was not allowed to transmit any political material, even in news bulletins. It was effectively gagged. At other times it included political items in magazines, special programmes and, of course, news bulletins. Yet its output was fragmented, satisfying neither the viewers nor the politicians.

It was understandable that the BBC should proceed with caution. Politicians were, and always had been, jealous of its power, and for a few years they prevented the broadcasting of any political controversy. The ban was modified in 1928 and even then the Corporation had to observe strict rules laid down by the political parties. A current affairs editor, Donald Edwards, told how an independent-minded politician who was kept off the air offered the BBC £100 out of his own pocket for the right to speak for half-an-hour on politics; the offer—by Winston Churchill—had to be rejected. But such restrictions could not be continued indefinitely. In fact some people later felt that the pendulum had swung too far the other way. There was so much political controversy throughout 1960 that there were complaints about 'argy-bargy' programmes and objections to the trivialisation of politics.

In the following year a new programme, *Gallery*, attempted to reflect political controversy without histrionics. I worked as associate editor of this programme for some time and became deeply interested in the love–hate relationship between politicians and broadcasters. They are suspicious of each other's power and jealous of their own. Collectively politicians are supreme, since Parliament can change the BBC's charter and veto a broadcast. But no government has ever exercised its power to ban, no doubt fearful of establishing a precedent which could lead to censorship by its successors. Individual politicians, conscious of television's power, seek to use it as an instrument of publicity for themselves and their party. Inevitably there is an underlying tension, especially between politicians and interviewers. On the rare occasions when interviewers went too far and hectored or were impolite to Members of Parliament there was a cry of anguish about the excessive power of the broadcasters. But these outbursts obscured the reality of an interviewer's need to probe, and if necessary to persist. Politicians should be able to deal effectively with fair but critical questions about their policies, and if some are unable to do so it is more a reflection on them than on the programme.

As I produced these programmes I became more deeply aware of the differences between back-bench MPs and television producers. Both wield power; but whereas the producer has regular and frequent access to a mass audience with his programmes, which most MPs do not, he does not express his own views. He produces the views of others. The MP is able to operate directly in Parliament, pressing for the implementation of policies he believes in. I began to regret that I had stayed so long in the BBC and I decided to try for a Parliamentary seat.

When I told the head of my department that I intended to try for a Parliamentary candidature he warned me that permission would probably be refused. My request went through various levels of the hierarchy until finally I was told to see Kenneth Adam, the Controller of Television. An old friend, who had been partly responsible for my joining the BBC, he said that I could not be given permission to become a Parliamentary candidate. As he gave me the gloomy news he offered a large cigar instead of a cup of tea and a biscuit. When I told him that I understood the situation I suspected that I saw a twinkle in his eye; he didn't inquire whether I still intended to seek a seat, and I never told him. I went back to my office and scanned the list of vacant Parliamentary seats.

I first applied for Neath, in South Wales, which was reputed to be in the gift of the Welsh miners and steelworkers. As I travelled by train through the valleys I felt that it was an alien land. For me Wales was the land of the Bevans and the Baverstocks, mercurial men who spoke English with a lilting accent and had been reared in a nationalist culture which, although British, was foreign to me. As a Lancashireman, I felt I could understand Yorkshire and the Midlands; Scotland perhaps, but Wales never.

At the selection conference there was no doubt that my prospects of gaining the seat were remote. I was not a Welshman, a mine-worker or a steelworker; but the reception I had from the conference was so warm and friendly that it gave me tremendous encouragement. Some of the men who voted for the successful candidate told me that they would like to see me in the House of Commons.

Within weeks two seats became vacant and I was short-listed for both of them. The first selection conference was at Barrow-in-Furness and the second, a week later, at Stoke-on-Trent. The Widnes Rugby Football team had played Barrow for years and I had passed through Stoke-on-Trent many times on my way from London to Widnes, so I felt no sense of remoteness as I had when I applied for Neath. At the Barrow selection conference my speech was well received and question time presented no insurmountable problems until I was asked if I would give an undertaking to spend every weekend up to the General Election electioneering in the constituency. This was impossible because my job at the BBC often involved weekend work, but I promised to campaign as frequently as possible. A section of the conference was not satisfied and, as they magnified the issue, I could feel support for me ebbing quickly. I was not selected, but I was far from discouraged.

At Stoke-on-Trent the candidates included a local man, a university lecturer, and a trade union leader; we chatted together in a small ante-room as each man took his turn to deliver a speech and answer questions. It was all so apparently casual, yet we knew that on the decision hung a Parliamentary career. Although my speech and answers to questions appeared to be well received, it was slightly disturbing to hear applause in the distance as other candidates spoke; we all pretended to ignore it as we indulged in small talk. When the votes had been counted the chairman came into the ante-room and told us that I had been selected. I was elated, although I tried not to show it too much. Now I was free to campaign for all the issues I felt so deeply about.

I celebrated with Pauline and the family and returned to the BBC the following day to give them the news. Despite the careful consideration which had been given to my request to seek a seat, and the firm rejection, they accepted the news blandly, even casually. Arrangements were immediately made for me to move to programmes which did not involve politics or current affairs; until the General Election I occupied myself with scientific programmes. It was a gesture of good will from the BBC, and I appreciated it. In fact they went further, and Huw Wheldon and some other executives gave a lunch in my honour after the election.

12

Entering Parliament

Polling day in the 1966 General Election—March 31st—promised to be a memorable day for me. Opinion polls were favourable to the Labour Party and in Stoke-on-Trent, South, I was defending a majority of 10,000. My supporters worked as if it was a marginal seat, giving my opponent no hope of a surprise victory through complacency. Sometimes loudspeakers broke down or posters arrived late but my agent, Bert Robinson, was unperturbed; he shared the general conviction that we would increase our majority to 12,000.

Although I had met Party workers at meetings since the selection conference, the election campaign was my first opportunity of working closely with them; they included some notable characters. The chairman, Sir Albert Bennett, a tall, handsome man with a dominating personality, outshone his political opponents and was leader of the City Council and a formidable spokesman until he died in 1972, aged 71. As chairman of my election meetings he was so devastating with hecklers that I almost felt redundant. Far from avoiding them, he sought them out and crushed them with scathing attacks; all I had to do was to pick up the pieces after he had finished.

Apart from a small group of Communists who followed me around, my meetings were mainly attended by enthusiastic supporters. I knew that the Conservative candidate would be suffering the same frustration as I had experienced in Finchley. This time he had to face massive opposition and I was the one who was confident of victory. It is so easy to be cool and confident from a position of overwhelming strength.

Our headquarters were the Labour Hall, a small, old building opposite the Town Hall, where I had been selected. Party workers spent many hours there each day folding my election addresses and putting them into envelopes, while I spent my days canvassing people in the streets and shopping centres, or touring with a loudspeaker van; in the evenings I addressed meetings throughout the constituency. Campaigning came naturally to me. I enjoyed meeting people and I slipped into the candidate's role as comfortably as into a tailor-made coat.

Despite its short life and narrow majority the Labour Government had some striking achievements to its credit. When it had taken office eighteen months earlier, the deficit on our overseas payments had been £750 million but this had been halved by the beginning of 1966. Even while struggling to free the country from this deficit, the Government had achieved record investment in schools, hospitals and the number of houses built. These were the basic issues of the campaign; the fun lay in tweaking the Tories when they offered alternatives. Why, if they were so good, had these panaceas not worked in the thirteen years they were in office? It was a difficult question for them to answer.

Pauline was anxious to play an active part in the election but everyone pressed her not to as she was shortly expecting our third baby. She came up for the last few days of the campaign. On polling day all my supporters turned out to maximise the vote, working energetically until the last possible moment. Because of an irritating convention in the city, votes were not counted until the following day, so when the booths closed the votes were locked away, while I went with Pauline and some friends to watch other people's results being announced on television.

Next day the count was almost a formality though I felt oddly apprehensive just before my result was announced, as if the whole thing was too good to be true. My majority was the forecast 12,000; at last I was going to Westminster—and on the crest of a great Labour Party wave. The Government increased its majority from three to ninety-seven and I anticipated a radical transformation of our society, for there seemed little to prevent the fulfilment of Labour's hopes after this dazzling electoral triumph.

The Queen opened the new Parliament on April 21st, 1966, amid the traditional pomp and ceremony, and although I was more concerned with the serious business to follow I had a special interest in the ritual. Watching the royal procession in the House of Lords was a small, white-haired old lady, utterly absorbed in the colourful pageantry. After all her years in Wellington Street, my mother had come to London to see the Queen. Still possessing that magical mixture of diffidence and personal warmth, Mam was aglow with excitement. It touched me deeply. She had been given a generous send-off in Widnes where Ken Merrifield drove her and my sister Helen to the station; the *Widnes Weekly News* photo-graphed her departure and reported her visit as its front-page lead story. I knew that it was an unforgettable day for her and it was a very happy one for me.

Later that morning I went to my first meeting of the Parliamentary Labour Party in Church House, Westminster. At this crowded and enthusiastic gathering Harold Wilson was given an ovation for winning a great victory. Jim Callaghan, the Chancellor of the Exchequer, said that while the Prime Minister had done his best for the Party, loyalty was a two-way process and he was entitled to it in the years ahead. As he spoke, I wondered what the reaction would be when the euphoria had evaporated and the Prime Minister had to make difficult and unpopular decisions. I pondered, too, on how the Tory leader, Edward Heath, would fare at his first meeting after electoral defeat, for it is not only the Americans who admire success.

That afternoon I went to the Chamber in good time and took stock of my new surroundings. They were not wholly unfamiliar, because I had watched debates from the gallery but the angle was different; instead of being an onlooker I was now involved. When the Chamber began to fill with Members I realised how small it was; I was conscious of an odd sense of intimacy.

We crowded jubilantly on the Government benches while our subdued opponents faced us. They were close; out of arms' reach, but not much more. In place of electoral battles from separate public platforms we were now set for years of political confrontation—practically eyeball to eyeball. The public gallery to our right seemed remote and irrelevant, while the Press gallery on our left, high above the Speaker's chair, seemed much closer. In fact it was the same distance from our benches as the public gallery. The illusion was because the Press, reporting and commenting on the proceedings, were intimately involved with the House.

A lobby correspondent told me that my predecessor, Ellis Smith, always sat at the end of the fourth bench, behind Ministers, just next to the gangway. He said I would be entitled to the seat so I decided to make it my regular place. As I sat watching the Chamber fill, conscious of a great sense of occasion in the new Parliament, an older Member approached and brusquely told me to move along. If he had asked, I would have obliged readily, but as it was I had no intention of moving; he persisted and we argued until the proceedings began. I was still adamant and he would not go elsewhere, so he sat on the floor at the side of my seat—an incident noticed by the Press, who commented on the awkwardness of some of the new Members.

The first business was to elect a new Speaker and Dr Horace King, who had served for the last six months of the old Parliament, was proposed by James Griffiths, a former Deputy Prime Minister. Griffiths, eloquent and sincere, made a speech which fitted the distinguished occasion. After Dr King had taken the Chair, the Loyal Address was moved. I was completely absorbed in the proceedings until a telephone message was passed to me along the crowded benches: Pauline had been taken to hospital and our baby was expected at any moment. I dashed away, arriving just in time to see her for a few minutes before being ushered out by a nurse, and shortly afterwards the doctor came to say that she had had a baby girl. That day, April 21st, 1966, I had a happy wife, three lovely children, and I stood on the threshold of an exciting Parliamentary career.

I had been so long on the sidelines that I was impatient to participate in the hurly-burly of Parliamentary life. But first I had to make my maiden speech. Some Members said the sooner the better; others suggested waiting some months until I was accustomed to the atmosphere. Most people counselled a non-controversial speech; a few felt this convention was outmoded. The question of a non-controversial speech was a controversial subject. I spoke on April 28th, just a week after the opening of Parliament and I defended the Government's prices and incomes policy, which was being strongly criticised at that time. Most of the speech was intended to be constructive but I could not resist attacking my opponents as 'breast-beating Tarzans who want to return to the economic jungle'. Unfortunately the critics of the prices and incomes policy were not confined to the Conservative benches—some were on ours. Later in the debate Woodrow Wyatt complimented me generously, which, after my clashes with him, I greatly appreciated.

I soon realised that while Parliamentary reputations were made on the floor of the House, influence was exercised elsewhere. In Committee and small subject-groups, reason replaced rhetoric. Accommodation took precedence over accusation and, while Party divisions were inevitable, the discussions were more constructive. There were also innumerable small cabals based on a mixture of common political outlook and personal friendship, and one often led to the other. New Labour Members were invited to meet Ministers, including the Prime Minister, in their private rooms for discussions. Some were useful, but the most significant were those which led to further meetings and sometimes alliances. I wished to avoid entanglement in any clique, although I wanted to be involved in the consultations.

The most influential gatherings were those of the Parliamentary Labour Party, held in a large Committee Room in an atmosphere strikingly different from the Chamber. There was none of the formality of Parliamentary debates where we had to refer to Members by their constituencies and follow long-established conventions and procedures. Party political conflict did not exist because we were all Members of the same Party; nevertheless there were often strong differences of opinion. I had heard of rancorous conflicts during the days of some early Labour leaders like Ramsay MacDonald; many Members had vivid recollections of the Party debates between Hugh Gaitskell and Aneurin Bevan in the fifties, when bitterness ran so deep that Party Members stopped speaking to each other. We had no such scenes at the meetings I attended, though divisions existed, particularly between the critical left-wing Tribune group who wanted faster progress towards an egalitarian society, and the majority of the Party whose first priority was support for the Labour Government. Despite my high regard for some of the men who demanded a more radical policy, I was convinced that Party divisions could be disastrous.

Surprisingly enough, one of the most serious disputes in the Parliamentary Party cut across those left-right lines. The Government's policy of maintaining military bases East of Suez was opposed by Christopher Mayhew, himself a right-winger, and at one of the most dramatic and crowded Party meetings he proposed a motion that was highly critical of the Government's policy. The Prime Minister rejected it and by insisting that 'the Government must govern' seemed to imply that it would be an issue of confidence in him. One of the most fiery characters in Parliament, Emanuel Shinwell, presided over the meeting. He was an authoritative chairman and after the motion was proposed he allowed no speaker from the floor to exceed five minutes, however famous or distinguished he might be. Anyone who attempted to do so was warned menacingly with a flourish of his gavel before he hammered him to order.

I was called in the debate and I opposed Mayhew's motion. He had spoken well and I disagreed with him more on the question of timing than of principle. I argued that divisions within a Party are an understandable and often necessary part of political life, but they delighted our enemies and dismayed our friends. Sometimes they could be dangerous and irreparably damaging. I asked for the withdrawal of the motion but Mayhew refused and it was eventually defeated. After the meeting I was congratulated by many Members of the Party and soon afterwards I met Albert Bennett who said that Bob Mellish, the Minister of Public Works, had told him it was a splendid speech; as it was my first effort, the compliment pleased me.

Delighted as I was by the generous response, it was ironically marred by the sadness of attending the funeral of a man who had vigorously supported my early efforts to enter the House of Commons. Nat Birch, the kindly Jewish orator from Finchley, had died a few days earlier and I left the exciting atmosphere of Westminster for Golders Green crematorium. The reception given to my speech at the Parliamentary Labour Party a few hours earlier had been a stirring experience, but the sorrow of Nat's family placed it in perspective.

During the next few months I extended my range of interests which included social services, disablement, industrial relations and broadcasting, and I was developing a new interest in foreign affairs. I wanted to feel my way before concentrating on a few major issues, but the dominant one became the Government's prices and incomes policy. Many attempts by previous Governments to establish such a policy had failed and for over a decade Britain had alternated between feverish bouts of inflation and deflation. The so-called stop–go cycle was inevitable with a fixed exchange rate, inadequate reserves and no policy to bring productivity, prices and incomes into balance. When I entered Parliament the need for such a policy was urgent since in the previous year earnings had risen 9·5 per cent, prices 5 per cent and production 1 per cent. At that time they seemed significant variations, and economists were predicting that our exports would be priced out of world markets and the country would face bankruptcy.

It was in these circumstances that the Government introduced the Prices and Incomes Bill in July 1966. This put the Prices and Incomes Board on a permanent basis and gave the Government statutory powers to demand early warning of intended price, or pay, increases. The Government could impose a standstill for one month while it considered whether to refer any proposed increase to the Board. If it did refer, it could impose a further standstill for three months.

I strongly supported the policy since new measures were essential if the stop–go cycle was to be broken. After the Board had considered a claim, trade unions and employers were free to act on their own judgement, so there was not such a significant restriction as some opponents of the Bill claimed. Nevertheless these clauses were highly controversial and in the second reading debate on July 14th some of our Labour colleagues were as critical as the Conservatives in opposing them. But worse was to come. Only six days after this stormy debate the Prime Minister announced emergency measures to deal with the economic crisis which had been sparked off by a seven-week seamen's strike. This stoppage, coupled with our steadily rising prices, led to speculation by overseas financiers, causing a heavy loss of sterling reserves. The Government's measures included a six-month freeze on prices and incomes. New clauses, giving power to impose this for twelve months, were tabled in the House of Commons. The stage was set for war between Labour Members.

The Bill was piloted through the Commons by George Brown, one of the most ebullient and colourful characters in the House; he was forceful and determined—so a tough and lively battle was inevitable. I was appointed to the Committee which examined the Bill clause by clause and line by line and we sat throughout the night for many arduous and wearying sessions. One of the most vociferous opponents of the Bill was Frank Cousins, former General Secretary of the mammoth Transport and General Workers Union. He had recently resigned as Minister of Technology and soon became leader of the dissentients on our benches.

It was no pleasure to be a backbencher on the Government side of this Committee because our votes were needed but our voices were not. The Minister and his deputies put forward each section of the Bill and fought it with the Opposition—or Frank Cousins. Contributions from Government backbenchers were discouraged because they delayed the Bill but this did not worry Cousins and he frequently attacked the Government. He had the courage of his convictions, but his continual sniping added to my frustration. In a debate on the floor of the House, I decided to attack him: I accused him of confusing long-term solutions with short-term necessities and of being unable or unwilling to see the relationship between wage inflation and the balance of payments. I claimed he was peddling panaceas which were one-third argument and two-thirds hogwash and I asked the House not to confuse stridency with sagacity, or volume with value. Some of his supporters objected strongly to this personal attack. The following day when I walked into the Committee meeting, Cousins sat fuming with anger; he called to me caustically to ask if I was now satisfied. I shrugged him aside and he never spoke to me again. Looking back I regret the incident. I wish I had dealt more with the issues and less with the man.

Occasional brief reports of my Parliamentary activities appeared in the Press but an incident occurred which pushed me into the national limelight overnight. A local news agency reporter in Stoke-on-Trent told me that one of my constituents had been arrested as a deserter, although he claimed he had been discharged from the Army. The man, Leslie Parkes, had been taken into custody by the local police, handed over to the Army, and imprisoned in a military barracks in Surrey. His outspoken protests had been widely reported in the Press and on television and when I arrived to visit him at the barracks I found a crowd of reporters and photographers waiting.

Parkes, with the marks of handcuffs on his wrists, said he had been manacled for a long time. He claimed that he had been discharged from the Army a few weeks earlier and that, although he had lost the discharge ticket, his colleagues in his unit in Germany could vouch for it. He was further upset by the condition of his cell, which he said was windowless with only a bed and no other furnishings.

I had been courteously though coolly received by the officer-in-charge and after hearing Parkes's allegations I asked if I could see the cell. Apparently taken aback by this request the officer said he would have to consult about it but after a telephone call, presumably to the Commanding Officer, he agreed. As I went with him across the parade ground he tried to march briskly but I was disinclined to trot at his side and walked at my usual pace. Conditions in the cell were just as bad as Parkes had described them. As I left the barracks I was surrounded by a crowd of journalists who were interested in the Army's treatment of a man who might not even be under its jurisdiction. The individual case became important because of the principle involved. Next day the story was splashed on the front pages.

I asked the Under-Secretary of State for Defence for the Army, James Boyden, to conduct an enquiry into Parkes's allegations and, meanwhile, to release him. Though he ordered the enquiry, he refused to let Parkes go. But public opinion was aroused, and when the Chief Constable of Stoke-on-Trent admitted that the police had arrested Parkes under false pretences, a major Parliamentary row was inevitable.

I applied for a Private Notice Question in the House of Commons, a Parliamentary device for raising an urgent matter of public concern. Normally oral questions are tabled a fortnight in advance but in special circumstances the Speaker can allow a question to be answered the same day. Many applications are made, few are granted. Mine was accepted though I did not learn until later that the Ministry of Defence strongly urged the Speaker to reject the Question. Just before it was due at 3.30 p.m. I saw the Minister, who still refused to release Parkes pending the result of the enquiry.

In a crowded House of Commons I rose to put my question. Although I was careful to avoid a general attack on the police and the Army, I criticised the handling of this individual case. Members on both sides of the House supported me but the Minister would not change his mind. After these exchanges I decided to apply for a writ of habeas corpus. I had emphasised throughout that I was not in a position to judge whether Parkes was guilty or innocent; but in view of the false arrest there was a strong case for releasing him pending the result of the enquiry. His solicitor arranged to come to London to discuss the issue of the writ.

Meanwhile a few Members were angry at what they regarded as an attack on the Army. Gerry Reynolds, who was second in command at the Ministry of Defence, felt deeply about it and I had some strong though friendly arguments with this fine man. But the MP who seemed most upset was George Wigg, the Paymaster-General: he never doubted that the Army was right and Parkes wrong, and he strongly objected to my handling of the case. When he met me in the Members' Lobby of the Commons we clashed angrily.

I had arranged to meet Parkes' solicitor at Euston station when he arrived from Stoke-on-Trent and as I waited on the platform I was surrounded by television cameramen and journalists. I stood rather self-consciously in a pool of floodlights while a curious crowd gathered around. When all the passengers had left the train I began to wonder where the solicitor had gone—but after a lengthy pause he stepped forward from the crowd where he had been cautiously watching. We saw Parkes and next day we went to a barrister's chambers to prepare our case. In the course of a long discussion I telephoned the War Office to clarify a point. They had been trying to find me all morning and an anxious official told me that the Minister of Defence, Dennis Healey, would make an important statement in the House that afternoon which I might welcome. It was as far as he would go but it was obvious that the tide of battle was turning.

I hurried back to the Commons in time to hear Healey say he had decided to wipe the slate clean and free Parkes. Some generous things were said by him and other MPs about the way I had conducted my constituent's case; there were even shouts of 'Good old Jack'. MPs claimed there was no need for an Ombudsman with Members like me around and an editorial in one of the newspapers the following day commented on my success. There was no danger of this praise going to my head but just to make sure someone wrote to me asking 'Who the bloody hell do you think you are to challenge the Army?'

However, the Minister's decision was by no means the end of the story and Gerry Reynolds told me that certain people were still 'gunning' for Parkes. A critical article was published in *The People*, and when, on television, Parkes repeated his story, some relatives claimed he had been lying all the time. After a further enquiry he was accused of perjury and found guilty. It was not a happy ending, but as I had refrained from judging the case throughout, I was content at achieving my limited and reasonable objective.

By this time my political career was flourishing and after just over a year in the House I was invited to become a Government Whip. Although I was flattered by the invitation after so short a time, I rejected it. Government Whips are responsible for discipline and ensuring that Members vote in divisions the right way and at the right time; a condition of the job is that they do not participate in debates. After so many years of producing BBC programmes which expressed other people's opinions, I was anxious not to be prevented from voicing my own. Another young MP, Eric Varley, was appointed instead. He later became the Parliamentary Private Secretary to the Prime Minister, and eventually Minister of State at the Ministry of Technology.

A few months later Michael Stewart, the Minister for Economic Affairs, invited me to be his Parliamentary Private Secretary. I had no idea that he was to become one of my staunchest friends in the difficult years ahead. He was an intelligent and compassionate Minister, experienced in many departments of State and held in high regard. At the Department of Economic Affairs he was dealing with intractable industrial problems and I felt able to make a useful contribution to his office because I had good relations with the trade union group; it was important that they should understand each other and consult regularly on industrial policy. I arranged meetings for them and although these were partly social occasions they were valuable in helping to avoid misunderstandings about some of his more controversial policies.

He gave me as much responsibility as he could, I enjoyed the work, and we developed an increasingly close relationship. When he became the Minister concerned with the long-term development of Social Policy, I transferred with him. Press speculations began to suggest that I would shortly become a Minister myself and after a government reshuffle, when two changes were announced without the Ministers being named, a newspaper reported that I had been appointed. I was in Widnes at the time and I telephoned a friend, Gerald Kaufman, who was the Prime Minister's personal assistant at 10 Downing Street, asking him if the report was true. When he told me that it was false, I was disappointed but by no means disconsolate. I was content to wait, and everyone seemed certain that before long I would get office. But it was not to be, and a few months afterwards I had the final operation which led to total deafness.

13

Resignation?

I was shattered when I lost the crucial remnant of hearing on the day I returned to the House of Commons. My plans were in ruins and I was plunged into a new, blank world, isolated from all external sound. The odds against my remaining in Parliament had been heavy for months but I had buoyed myself with hope while taking the crash course in lip-reading. Now the pressures had proved too great. I was mentally and physically exhausted from forcing myself so hard immediately after the illness, then failing the vital test. Success would have been a psychological boost—a springboard for further advance. But I could not build my life on what might have been. I had to live with the diametric difference between success and failure.

If only a job had been involved I would have been disappointed but not desperate. The problem was infinitely more complex and profound. I was cut off from mankind, surrounded by an invisible, inpenetrable barrier. I could see people clearly, but they belonged to a different world—a world of talk, of music and laughter. I could hardly believe I would never hear again. I tried pressing a radio to the side of my head in a vain attempt to make contact; when I turned the volume to full pitch I could only feel a delicate vibration as the set trembled. It was undeniable confirmation that although sound existed it was not for me.

That fragile wisp of hearing had maintained for me a slender contact with the ordinary world; it had given some sense of reality, a hint of that background of sound which, to a normal person, is so familiar as to be unnoticed. Without it, life was eerie; people appeared suddenly at my side, doors banged noiselessly, dogs barked soundlessly and heavy traffic glided silently past me. Friends chatted gaily in total silence.

The greatest deprivation was being unable to hear the human voice. Casual conversation—the common currency of everyday life—repartee or even a passing joke were things of the past; all I could manage to understand were simple messages spoken very slowly. Even talking to Pauline and the children had become almost impossible. This above all made me realise just how much was lost. Minute as it was, the residual hearing had been a vital adjunct to lip-reading, for the vague sounds had helped to make lip movements comprehensible to some extent: now, with total silence, they had become meaningless. The most experienced and skilful lip-readers invariably encounter difficulties, but I was new to the subject and found most people impossible to understand, even when they spoke clearly. I was struggling like a newly caught bird in a foolproof cage.

Had I been alone, I would almost certainly have despaired because the exhaustion was exacerbated by unfathomable depths of depression. I felt isolated, but I was not alone, as throughout that time Pauline never left my side. She spoke clearly and, incredibly, optimistically about the future. There were many better jobs than being a Member of Parliament, she said, and I could do them better than anyone: she reminded me of the chance that *some* hearing might return and that was the faint hope we clung to. Pauline telephoned the Liverpool surgeon and although he was not optimistic he prescribed rest and further drugs. I swallowed them faithfully for a week but this time they failed to restore the slightest hearing. As a final resort we went to see another consultant in a London hospital. He examined my ears, then simply looked at me and shook his head. It was the end of our hopes; together we left with that odd mixture of despair tinged with relief when one knows the worst, although the worst now had to be faced.

There was an atmosphere of quiet crisis at home and all the family was aware of it. At the end of a traumatic week we knew that I had to leave Parliament and pick up the threads of a new, silent world as best I could. I wrote to the chairman of my constituency Party, Sir Albert Bennett, telling him that I had no alternative but to resign. It was a simple message. I added that though I was young for memories I would always remember with pleasure my time as the Member for Stoke-on-Trent, South. Having written the letter I let it lie on my desk for the rest of the day. In the early evening I posted it with a sense of reluctant finality. I felt exhausted in a world of limitless despondency. I had been extremely happy in the House of Commons and had hoped to make a constructive contribution. Now I was looking for a job. None but the brave would employ a former politician who was totally deaf, and my family was obviously going to face serious economic problems. That night I wrote a batch of letters to people I knew, asking about jobs. I resolved the conflict between my wish to avoid asking favours and the need to provide for my family by saying in every letter that I would understand if they felt that in their particular field deafness was a major handicap.

The news of my resignation emerged in a strange way. The *Evening Sentinel*, the local newspaper in Stoke-on-Trent, had always been scrupulously fair to me. It is a newspaper with high professional standards, always leavening its criticism with a touch of humanity; it could differ without damning. I appreciated this fairness and as a final gesture before leaving the constituency gave the *Sentinel* the news as an exclusive story. Pauline telephoned it to Peter Rose, the paper's Lobby correspondent, who thanked her, and expressed his personal regret. Later in the morning Will Stewart, the London editor of the newspaper group, telephoned to say it was the saddest exclusive he had ever had for the paper. It was through him that I first became interested in campaigning in Parliament for the disabled, and now I was resigning because I was disabled.

The story was published in Stoke-on-Trent in mid-afternoon, a few hours after Sir Albert Bennett should have received my letter. I heard later that it did not arrive until the following day and he only learned of my decision when the *Sentinel* telephoned him for comment. He gave a non-committal statement. The news was now public and Pauline discussed it on the telephone with a Press Association correspondent in the constituency, but somehow it did not reach the London office. It was only after nine o'clock that night that the London office of the agency telephoned to say they had just got the story from 'another source' and asked if we could confirm it.

The message went on the news at 9.30 p.m. and from 9.35 p.m. there was a stream of telephone calls from the House of Commons. Everyone wanted me to carry on. It was touching but futile; I assumed they thought I was merely hard of hearing and they did not realise the fundamental difference between that and total deafness. Their messages showed the quality of the friends and colleagues I was being forced to leave, but they did nothing for my peace of mind.

The following day there were more telephone calls and two Members of Parliament, Eric Ogden and Michael McGuire, arranged to come and see me at my home in a few days' time. Although I appreciated the gesture, I felt that there could be only one conclusion to the discussion. Carrying on as a totally deaf

Member of Parliament was out of the question, despite the goodwill of my colleagues. Apart from the personal problems involved, I had been chosen as an MP with all his faculties and it would be presumptuous now to stay.

The Times carried a sympathetic story about my resignation and reading the *Stoke Sentinel* editorial was like reading my own obituary; they were generous words, but it was an unnerving experience. One of the telephone calls that morning was from a producer on the BBC's *World at One* programme. He wanted an interview and after some hesitation I agreed, although I explained it would be necessary to let me have advance notice of the questions. I had frequently broadcast before but I never arrived at a studio with such trepidation as I did that morning. Pauline came along to help if necessary. The interviewer, William Hardcastle, took it all in his stride and in the programme I tried to explain as coolly as possible how I felt about the situation. His last question was interesting and significant: 'Even though you are deaf, would you stay on if you were pressed strongly enough?' I thought not, but a seed had been planted in my mind. Were all the messages I had received merely expressions of sympathy, or did people really believe I could stay on? I didn't really know, nor did Pauline, but as we walked out of Broadcasting House something had subtly changed—it was as if a nerve suddenly flickered slightly in an apparently dead body.

That night we had dinner at home with an old friend, Stephen Bonarjee, with whom I had worked at the BBC. He was our first visitor from outside the family and we welcomed the opportunity to discuss our problems with him. I had wondered whether to cancel the date, which had been made before my total deafness. Perhaps he too feared an embarrassing evening, but in the event it was pleasant and stimulating. Since we valued his judgement we told him of the tiny flicker of hope that had been revived; his reaction was interesting. He paused, thought for a moment, then said that 'it might well be possible' to stay in the House of Commons. 'Yes', he added after reflection, 'it might well work.'

When he had gone Pauline and I talked long into the night. Although the hope of a miracle to save my hearing had vanished there seemed now to be a slender chance that I could return to Parliament *despite* being totally deaf. We decided to see how things developed—and laughed at my suggestion that we should play it by ear.

Next day there was another flood of telephone calls and letters from constituents and Parliamentary colleagues. I knew that the Government was passing through an unpopular phase and my electoral majority was not as safe as the figure of 12,000 suggested; but even political opponents urged me to stay on. One of the kindest letters of all came from Iain Macleod. Shortly afterwards the Government Chief Whip, John Silkin, wrote to say he had felt at first that I had no alternative to resigning but had changed his mind after careful consideration. He said that he had been approached by a large number of MPs who felt I should stay. His view was important for he was ideally placed to judge the mood and feelings of Members. We looked forward to hearing more from Eric Ogden and Michael McGuire, though not without some apprehension. Every encounter was a strain for me and I felt strangely diminished when meeting people I had known before I was deaf. Fortunately the obviously sincere goodwill of the two MPs carried us over the initial difficulties on arrival; they said everyone agreed that deafness was no insuperable problem to remaining in the Commons. A few days later my Parliamentary colleagues from Stoke-on-Trent, John Forrester and Bob Cant, confirmed what we had already been told about opinion in the House, adding that local people in my constituency were also anxious for me to stay. This was a crucial consideration; it was obviously time to visit Stoke-on-Trent.

But first something happened which influenced me deeply. Professor Peter Townsend, one of Britain's most distinguished sociologists, and his wife, Ruth, told us they felt strongly that I should remain in Parliament and put forward a reason which had not been advanced before. They said that in addition to my being able to help disabled people, it would benefit Parliament to have a disabled person in its midst with practical and personal experience of disability. Sir Ian Fraser, who had served for years as a blind MP, was mentioned as a notable example of this. I had known the Townsends at Cambridge and although I had lost touch over the years I held them in affection and esteem.

Peter's reputation as a pioneer of sociological studies made his opinion an influential one. He wrote to *The Times* and the *Evening Sentinel*, saying that despite my disability I could still make an effective contribution in Parliament. His intervention was significant because it authoritatively contradicted the widely held belief that disabled people were only fit for a few simple, specialised jobs. He made people think again about such a situation as mine, and I appreciated his initiative.

A few days later we had an anxious journey to Stoke-on-Trent. The tidal wave of goodwill was fine, but we were now to meet leaders of the constituency Party to discuss my future and I would be unable to hear a word they said. When we arrived there was a headline in the local paper '*Jack Must Stay*' *Chorus Swells*. The story quoted Professor Townsend and others who felt as he did. After a friendly welcome from an informal group of Party workers, we went into a small office to talk with Sir Albert Bennett. He explained, slowly and clearly, that though the decision rested not with him but with the local Party he personally felt that I was capable of representing the constituency in the House of Commons, and that I had a duty to stay on. He was eloquent, forceful and somehow, at the same time, gentle and understanding. Eventually, after a slow and lengthy discussion I agreed that if the Party wanted me to stay I would reconsider my decision to resign.

Next day the *Sentinel* carried a photograph of Pauline and me among Party workers and a guarded comment from Sir Albert saying that a statement would be made later.

In Parliament, and in my constituency Party, the omens were promising but I wondered how the public of Stoke-on-Trent would feel about being represented by a totally deaf MP. We went to see Bernard Sandall, one of the best-informed men on the *Evening Sentinel*. He is a reserved, thoughtful and intelligent man whose judgement commands tremendous respect in the Potteries. He affirmed that I would have the support of my constituents if I carried on, though I felt he was painfully aware of my dilemma. As we drove back to London we began to realise that the minor miracle was now a distinct possibility. Pauline drove most of the way as I was still exhausted, but instead of sitting in silence as before she fixed a mirror to the windscreen so that I could see to lip-read her. Although she had to speak very slowly and clearly, we were beginning to stumble back towards some kind of normality. We felt confused but much more hopeful.

However, I was under no illusion about the difficulties if I was to return to the House. I sensed that the problem would be even more intractable and complicated than anyone could visualise. Even conversation with Pauline, the most patient and clear speaker, was a strain. There were many busy people in Parliament, some of whom spoke like machine-guns. Would they have the time or make the effort to accommodate me? Would I be able to follow the debates adequately? Would it be possible to understand my constituents as they explained their problems? How great a physical and nervous strain would it be? Could I justify the confidence placed in me? Above all, could I make a useful contribution and maintain my self-respect? These were some of the questions which worried me as we travelled back to London to await the outcome of this extraordinary situation.

A few days later I was invited to discuss the problem with the Prime Minister at the House of Commons. It was another of what was becoming a series of ordeals. I felt bewildered as Pauline and I drove into New Palace Yard because it was only a few weeks before that I had decided never to enter the Commons again as it would evoke too many thoughts of what might have been. Yet there I was—neither a visitor nor a normal Member, for I had given notice of my resignation. We were escorted to Harold Wilson's room by his Parliamentary Private Secretary, Harold Davies, the genial, rotund Member for Leek, the constituency adjoining mine. I knew that the Prime Minister would be aware of my problem because Harold Davies had been present at the informal meeting in Stoke-on-Trent, though he stayed discreetly in the background.

My political future was the subject of that discussion, but what was fascinating was the way it was discussed. Harold Wilson behaved as if it were an ordinary conversation. Instead of addressing Pauline and talking through her, as so many people had already begun to do, he spoke directly to me. Because he was not embarrassed I felt relatively at ease, although I could not understand what he said. After each comment or question Pauline, who was quite unflustered, repeated his words for me and the conversation went smoothly. Urging me to stay in Parliament, he said he would be glad to help in any way he could. I was grateful and told him that I thought I would stay if the constituency Party decided that they wanted me to.

In the meantime I began to see some of the people whom I had asked about jobs. Many of them, like Sir Hugh Greene, the Director General of the BBC, Cecil King, Chairman of the International Printing Corporation, and Lord Cooper, General Secretary of my union, had replied immediately asking me to go and talk with them or some of their senior staff. I had also received kind, spontaneous letters from other people like Richard Bailey, the Director of

Political and Economic Planning, and G. D. N. Worswick of the National Institute of Economic and Social Research. The discussions were encouraging. At the BBC, Kenneth Lamb, who was in charge of the Secretariat, said they were anxious to find me a job I could not only do efficiently but would also enjoy doing. We discussed various possibilities which were to be pursued when my personal situation had clarified.

Cecil King had suggested that I should see Edward Pickering, his executive director. As we walked into his office in the *Daily Mirror* building he was just finishing a meeting with Hugh Cudlipp and one or two other people. We met them briefly, then discussed my prospects with Mr Pickering. A quiet, friendly man, he said he would be glad to employ me in labour relations because of my experience in that field. I was grateful and arranged a further meeting with him, but shortly afterwards it was announced that Cecil King had been deposed from the chairmanship of IPC and that Hugh Cudlipp had taken over. I did not know if this would affect the offer made to me but Edward Pickering assured me that it remained open. When I explained the possibility of my return to the House he said he would still be willing to use my services on a part-time basis. Although I did not accept, I appreciated this kind offer.

When we went to see Lord Cooper at the Union's head office in Claygate, Surrey, we were kept waiting in an outer office for half an hour. As the minutes ticked by, I felt more like a supplicant than an applicant. I wondered if he might be reluctant to discuss the problem —and I could understand that—but when at last the door was flung open he breezed in and greeted me warmly. The reason for the delay was a sudden strike which he was trying to settle. Without hesitation he offered to give me a job as soon as he had discussed it with his colleagues. So the economic threat receded, though I was still uncertain about my future.

The continuing flow of letters and messages of support had a great influence on me, strengthening my decision to stay in Parliament if invited by the local Party. Although I was under no illusion about the magnitude of the task, my mind was finally made up. But what would their decision be? The answer was to be given at a special conference at the Labour Hall in Stoke-on-Trent. When Sir Albert Bennett came to see us before the meeting, he was properly non-committal about the likely outcome, but we knew that he was in favour of my staying. He felt it was better if the Party made their decision in my absence and of course he was right. Pauline and I arranged to wait in the Working Men's Club nearby in case I was wanted for questioning. The meeting began at 7.30 p.m. I ordered a drink for Pauline and myself and settled down for an anxious wait; but within five minutes some delegates came from the meeting to tell us that a unanimous resolution had been passed inviting me to stay as their Member of Parliament. It was one of the rare happy moments I had known since going deaf.

Pauline and I joined the meeting and were greeted enthusiastically, even emotionally, as we entered. Grateful for their support, I made a short speech of acceptance: a wholly inadequate expression of my feelings. Ahead lay a challenging, even intimidating, task. My Parliamentary career, to which I seemed temperamentally suited, was one I enjoyed, and I should have been rejoicing. Yet the nagging reservation remained—that I might be imposing an unbearable strain on myself, on top of the already crushing burden of deafness and tinnitus. But I wanted to try, hoping that from the despair of the past and the exhaustion of the present, a more promising future would emerge.

The BBC had expressed interest when they heard about the special conference at Stoke-on-Trent and they wanted to interview me. Michael Barratt, one of their reporters, came with a camera crew to my home. We were old friends who had worked together in television but when he arrived he was obviously apprehensive about how to conduct the interview. After the handshake and welcome he seemed nonplussed. 'How do I talk to you?' he asked. Pauline and I laughed at this discomfiture but he took it in good part. I was relieved to notice from these opening words that he was not too difficult to lip-read; we discussed the general line of questions together before recording the interview in our living room. Somehow I was able to follow the series of questions and Michael seemed satisfied with the interview; he never admitted it but I suspect my voice sounded a bit strangled. Some months later, when I appeared on television, one of my colleagues said that my voice was 'better than on the *24 Hours* programme'!

The transmission of the interview coincided with an important Division. I did not want to meet colleagues on that occasion, and although I was in the precincts to register my vote, I was excused from the Lobbies. While other members voted, I sat in the Chief Whip's office with Pauline and watched the programme. An official from the Whip's office, who also watched, seemed touched by my perversity in staying on despite well-meaning advice to take a quiet job and have an easy life. Was I being perverse? I didn't know. I was instinctively fighting back, but there was nothing noble about that. It was a reaction determined in part by my nature and also by my upbringing.

Whatever the reason, I was now back in politics. The first stage of the battle had been so all-consuming that it carried me over the traumatic shock of becoming deaf; the rest was to unfold in the years ahead. That night Pauline and I were content, for we had passed a landmark together. The challenge of the future could not be measured; I was facing a unique situation, about to journey into uncharted territory.

14

The Silent House

Returning to the House of Commons without any hearing was a hazardous undertaking. On the last occasion I had clung to a wisp of sound; this time I had nothing to cling to. I was enveloped in a shroud of silence from which there was no escape. My previous attempt to return to the House had ended in disaster and left its mark. Now I was about to try again—with even less confidence.

Since losing my hearing I had relied on Pauline to help with people who could neither comprehend nor deal with deafness. Speaking clearly for me, she eased the pressure of eye-strain and ensured that I understood the conversations. She firmly refused to allow people to ignore me while they talked to her—a natural tendency for those who could not be bothered to speak clearly. Whoever they were, working men or Cabinet Ministers, if they tended to push me out of the conversations in those early days they would be told politely but firmly: 'Talk to Jack.' But now I was going alone to the House of Commons. No doubt arrangements could have been made for her to accompany me. But I didn't want that, partly because of her domestic responsibilities but mainly because I was determined to be as independent as possible in my role as a Member of Parliament.

It was a gamble, for if I failed I would be forced out of politics. Would I be able to establish a narrow bridgehead of independence from which I could advance as my lip-reading improved? To do so would require the understanding and co-operation of my colleagues. They were busy people, often involved in controversial matters which were not designed to keep the mercury low. If I was to play an active part I must engage in these controversies, which could be as emotionally charged between Party colleagues as between political opponents. Was it reasonable to hope for understanding while speaking as frankly and vigorously as I had in the past? Dampening the fire of controversy would be out of character for me, and it would do less than justice to the issues.

At least this time Members would be aware of my disability. They all knew I was totally deaf and dependent on lip-reading—yet they wanted me to return. But did they fully appreciate the enormity of the problem? Despite their letters of encouragement urging me to return would they be shocked when confronted with a colleague who required painstaking patience before being able to understand a limping dialogue? Would I be able to establish any semblance of ordinary relationships with my colleagues and officials of the House?

Understanding debates was important, but other occasions, previously taken for granted, would now present major problems. To check a point made in debates I could always read Hansard, the Official Report, but there is no report of those informal discussions in corridors and tea-rooms which are as important to political understanding as formal debates. Discussions over a meal would be difficult, partly because of inadequate lip-reading but also because I had to look at my plate to eat and this could cause me to lose the tenuous thread of comprehension. I might become an albatross around the necks of my colleagues, or an odd man out on my own.

As I left for the House, Pauline and I smiled reassurance to each other. We had discussed every detail of the problems, but now I was on my own. I drove through uncannily silent traffic in a subdued mood, as if reserving my energies for what lay ahead; I felt like a spring coiled for action, without any idea what action would be required. As I walked through the Members' entrance I was approached by a policeman with a thick, bushy moustache. Normally no one would be more difficult to lip-read, but he said slowly and clearly 'Welcome back sir'. They were the first words spoken to me on my return and, because of his consideration, I understood them.

In the Members' Lobby I was surrounded by friends and well-wishers. I did not pretend to understand all they said and no one launched into a detailed conversation. It was a unique atmosphere compounded of extraordinary warmth, a little bewilderment and the faintest suggestion of embarrassment. Everyone wanted to welcome me yet no one knew how to say it other than in the simplest terms. I dallied for only a few moments before going into the Chamber.

There is no ideal seat for a lip-reader in the House of Commons. Long benches facing each other along the Chamber are divided by a gangway. The front benches above the gangway are for Ministers on one side and Opposition leaders on the other. Those behind them, and below the gangway, including the front bench, are for backbenchers. I thought my best position would be at the far end of our front bench below the gangway; I could then pivot round and see both sides. The redoubtable Bessie Braddock, who had visited me in the Liverpool hospital, always sat there but when I wrote to her about it she assured me there would be no problem.

It was Question Time when I walked in and the front bench was full so I stood undecided at the Bar of the House. Until a Member crosses this line near the end of the Chamber he is technically not in the House and unable, therefore, to take part in the proceedings. The usual fusillade of questions was being fired at Ministers and I was anxious to avoid interrupting by trying to squeeze on to the crowded bench. I was uncomfortably aware that many Members from both sides were beginning to look at me, but the moment Bessie Braddock spotted me she turned to the crowded bench and called 'Push up'. She gave them a friendly shove as she spoke and as she weighed at least fifteen stone the effect was dramatic. A space was provided where she had been sitting a moment ago. She patted it in welcome and I thankfully slid into it, shielded to some extent by her massive maternal frame from the full gaze of the House.

After a few moments I tried to lip-read. I had not expected to understand much but the reality was a chilling experience. I understood very little of what was said and, to add to my discomfort, I had no idea where to look. By the time I had swivelled round to locate a speaker he would be half way through his question; a brief one would be finished before I could start to make any sense of it.

This did not seem like the Chamber where I had vigorously interrupted other speakers and impatiently waited my turn to speak. It was transformed into a mysterious, menacing arena where I could be trapped into misunderstanding the arguments and passions which swiftly ebbed and flowed. It would be all too easy to make a fool of myself: somehow I had to make sense out of this silence and as I sat there I reflected on the daunting prospect.

I became conscious for the first time of the shifting patterns of light in the Chamber. The high windows above the Distinguished Strangers' Gallery caught and reflected the slightest change of sunlight on this fitfully cloudy day. As shadows flitted across the faces I was trying to lip-read they made a difficult task nearly impossible. I tried to dispel the thought that it seemed symbolic of the sun setting on my political career.

Soon my spirits drooped and my eyes grew tired; I left the Chamber and went into the tea-room. There, touched by warmth and friendship, I felt my depression lifting, despite the problems. Conversation was not easy but it was not impossible, because colleagues were mainly enquiring about my personal situation and if they had to repeat themselves they were ready to do so. The House of Commons is a remarkable institution; its Members are individually diverse but collectively they act in subtle unity. Crushing to anyone who offends against their canons, they can sometimes lavish affection which is powerful and moving. I was the fortunate recipient of this immense goodwill at a time when I needed it most.

That evening at a meeting of the Parliamentary Labour Party, the main item on the agenda was a proposal to rebuke a group who had refused to accept a majority decision; I decided to see if valour was the better part of discretion and I intervened in the debate. Although I grasped only a little of the opening speech I used that fragment as a peg on which to hang a speech of my own. I regretted the group's action but supported a proposal that the issue be dropped. The speech was well received, but I knew that the applause was more in the nature of a welcome back.

At the end of the day I went home weary but cautiously optimistic. My welcome in the House had been encouraging and Pauline typically focused on this in our discussions that night, but the massive problems ahead still seemed to stretch to infinity. The strain I had been under since becoming deaf had exhausted me and my eyes were perpetually shadowed. I was rarely able to relax, for lip-reading always demanded concentration and to this burden was now added great psychological pressure. During the past few months I had not been able to keep up with fast-moving political events but now I had returned I could not operate in a political vacuum; I had to begin reading about issues and developments, and to acquaint myself with current controversies. My personal batteries were low, yet I had to press on, pick up the threads, continue my constituency work, participate in the House of Commons, and simultaneously try to improve my lip-reading.

Attendance at the House is controlled by the Whips, whose job it is to ensure that voting strength is maintained in Divisions. If a Member has to be away for any pressing reason they arrange to 'pair' him with a Member of the opposing Party so that the relative strength of each side is unchanged. I found at that time—and have ever since—that, contrary to popular myths, the Parliamentary Labour Party Whips are men of deep understanding. They are often caricatured as hatchet men and it is in the nature of their job to be firm, yet they eased my problems and the only pressure they exerted was to make sure I did not overwork.

During the weeks and months that followed, I was gradually compelled to face the realities of my situation. Making contact with other Members was a remarkable experience. Whenever I attempted a conversation with them there was always an invisible but impenetrable barrier between us. Invariably conversation began affably but ended in confusion or sometimes embarrassment. If they could not make themselves understood there was little left to do but jot down a note. Sometimes I would pretend I had followed and nod acknowledgement, but this created a sense of mutual uncertainty, no better than a simple acknowledgement of my failure to understand. It was an incredible situation to enjoy so much warmth and affection, yet be unable to make meaningful human contacts.

The major problems I had foreseen when trying to decide whether to stay in Parliament were now daily realities. After a few difficult encounters, many Members whom I had difficulty in lip-reading were still pleasantly disposed but they made no further attempt at conversation; this was partly to avoid embarrassing me but mainly because they themselves were embarrassed. The difficulties of conversation were so great in those early days that even some men of great goodwill preferred not to face them.

On one occasion in the tea-room I took my cup of tea to a table to join four friends. When one of them asked me a question which I could not understand, the others repeated it for me but I was still unable to lip-read it. They paused while one of them wrote it down and I was aware that the easy-going conversation they had been enjoying before my arrival was now disrupted. When I answered the written question it was understandable that none of them should risk a repeat performance by asking another. Within a few moments two of them left and after a brief pause the others explained that they had to go because of pressing engagements. They were genuinely sorry and I understood, but it was small solace as I sat alone drinking my tea.

Human nature being what it is, my relationships with many Members were inevitably eroded by deafness. The first indications were when casual suggestions to have a drink or dinner were equally casually dropped. Some people shied away from our formerly close contact. I did not blame them; they were simply reacting to a problem in their own individual way. They were not unfriendly; they smiled and nodded when passing me in the House—but the warmth had vanished. I missed it more deeply and more sadly than I cared to show.

Fortunately at that time there were a small number of people I could always rely on, no matter how great the difficulties. Alfred Morris stood out as the most considerate man in the House of Commons—and his unstinting generosity was to mean even more to me later. William Hamilton, one of the most formidable and forbidding Parliamentarians, was always available to help. Tough, austere and biting in debate, he proved to be one of my most staunch and gentle allies. When John Golding was elected for Newcastle-under-Lyme, he became as persistent in offering aid as in asking Parliamentary Questions. Gordon Oakes, from Widnes (then representing Bolton West, later MP for Widnes) refused to allow my deafness to interfere with an old friendship. My Parliamentary colleagues from Stoke-on-Trent, John Forrester and Bob Cant, spoke clearly and at meetings with deputations John Forrester always sat next to me and made notes to supplement my lip-reading. I appreciated his unselfish efforts, and his kindness greatly eased my difficulties. At meetings of the Parliamentary Labour Party I could always depend on Joe Ashton, the Member for Bassetlaw, to make notes. Whenever I made a speech he would jot down an encouraging comment about my voice or a compliment on my delivery, although he often disagreed with my views. And there were one or two relatively new friends, like Lewis Carter-Jones, the Member for Eccles, who made great efforts to establish contact and show their willingness to help.

Michael Stewart was now Foreign Secretary again and though he was exceptionally busy he invited Pauline and me down for the day to his official weekend residence at Dorneywood. When we arrived at this beautiful house, deep in the Buckinghamshire countryside, I wondered if deafness would affect my relationship with him as it had with so many others. He is a self-effacing personality, behind whose quiet demeanour lies a resolute character. When I was his Parliamentary Private Secretary he tolerated a certain flamboyance and allowed me to organise affairs at social functions while he carried on discussions with the guests. I had now lost some of my vitality, but within minutes of our meeting we were talking animatedly, pausing only for him to repeat slowly any sentences I found difficult.

After lunch we went for a walk which developed into a procession, with Michael and me together, followed by Pauline and Michael's wife, Mary, and the personal detective trailing discreetly behind. I had to try to understand Michael's conversation without any prompting from Pauline. Walking and talking while lip-reading can be hazardous, because it is impossible to look ahead all the time. When our conversation became too difficult we would stop to clarify a sentence while the detective would pause about ten yards behind us. I wondered what he thought of the Foreign Secretary's guest who stumbled through the woods, occasionally colliding with trees. I later learned that he was on friendly terms with Michael and understood the situation. It was an odd experience but I was immensely encouraged and stimulated by Michael's kindness. It was on such thoughtful actions that I began to rebuild my flagging self-confidence.

In the House of Commons the Speaker's attitude was important; if he had lacked understanding my difficulties would have been greater. Speaker King was a firm and sometimes impatient man who allowed no one to delay Parliamentary business. Fortunately for me he proved to be also a most thoughtful man who took great trouble to ease my way back. I met him for the first time after my return at a formal reception in his palatial apartments. I joined the queue to be received and when I reached him he dropped protocol and substituted for the formal handshake, a warm and long embrace. It was the first time I had ever been embraced by a man but I greatly appreciated the gesture. He promised to let me know in advance whether I was to be called in debates, so that I could avoid the eye-strain of sitting watching and waiting from mid-afternoon until late at night. On the occasions when he told me I would not be called I did not know whether to be pleased to have avoided eye-strain or sorry I had prepared a speech in vain.

Some difficult situations were unavoidable. I found the crowded Division Lobby the loneliest place in the Commons. It was always packed with Members but in those early days few came to talk to me. Apart from the inadequacy of my lip-reading, the noise level was high in the Lobby and it was difficult to adjust my voice, which hardly made for relaxed conversation. I usually passed through, trying to look at ease, while moving forward slowly with the drifting crowd. There can be no more demoralising sense of isolation than to be alone in a crowd.

These incidents had a desolating effect in the months after my return to the House; there were others which under normal circumstances I could have brushed aside as of no consequence. The number of social invitations I now received fell dramatically. Some of my former colleagues, or their wives, discreetly amended their guest lists. Invitations to formal and informal lunches, dinners and parties became notably scarce. I tried not to care too much about this and the real consolation was that the quality of my friendships was more important than the quantity. Those colleagues whose attitudes never changed or wavered can have no idea how much it meant to me.

Such problems arose partly because at first deafness pushed me out of the main stream of politics; in addition to difficulties of communication, I had less to talk about with my colleagues. There was little point in asking me what I thought of a speech they knew I had not heard and were probably reluctant to ask if I had lip-read. This was only a passing phase, but it was in marked contrast to my experience before I was deaf. Then my judgement was respected, and although my views were not always accepted, they were often sought by Parliamentary colleagues and political journalists. Now I could only wait for my lip-reading to improve.

The simplest jobs had become difficult; even asking the clerks questions about procedure posed problems. Complicated answers could only be given by slow, patient explanation or by writing the whole thing out in longhand. Officials were always helpful but I was anxious to avoid putting them to excessive trouble, so I found these encounters embarrassing. Yet there was no escape if I was to resist the temptation of opting out.

Some problems were more easily solved than I anticipated. I had expected to miss important Divisions because of being unable to hear the bell, but this never happened; I could usually detect a surge of movement in any part of the Palace of Westminster. As soon as three or four Members moved briskly in the direction of the Division Lobbies I would check the television prompters and confirm there was a Division. Sometimes colleagues working nearby would see that I was reading or writing and had failed to notice the movement of Members. They invariably let me know, and Conservative Members often smiled as they nudged me to go and vote against them.

Parliamentary questions posed difficulties since failure to lip-read replies would result in asking the wrong supplementary question. I therefore arranged to receive from Ministers a draft of their initial answer, though this still meant I had to lip-read the reply to my supplementary. It was more difficult when I intervened in other

Members' questions. If I missed a question or answer I could easily misconstrue the situation or be repetitious, so I occasionally asked colleagues to make a note for me before I intervened, but this created almost as many difficulties as it solved. Question time requires speedy reflexes, as nine or ten Members may jump up the moment a Minister sits down. While I was reading the note of the Minister's reply, my colleagues were on their feet and one would be called by the time I looked up. I had to draw a fine line between glancing at notes and swift lip-reading, with a preference for the latter if I could manage it.

The difficulty of making telephone calls and receiving messages was solved by the perceptive kindness and efficiency of Miss Kay Andrews of the Library staff. She recognised the problem and volunteered to help me because she realised I was reluctant to ask. If she happened to be otherwise engaged, other members of the Library staff or the police would assist me.

No matter how kind people were, the shock of total deafness reverberated daily for many months and shook me every day I entered the House of Commons. Whenever I walked into the Chamber I was struck by the absolute silence of the greatest debating forum in the land. I had no alternative but to join in as best I could, though my contribution was more limited than in earlier days. I felt at this time that I was only on the periphery of Parliament. I was slowly and hesitantly trying to understand this remarkable state of affairs and come to terms with it.

But one day, out of the blue, I was invited to propose a Ten-Minute-Rule Bill. This is a Parliamentary device which enables a Member to present the case for a change in the law. A Bill is prepared by the Member; supporters who may have campaigned on the subject or shown a special interest, add their names, and it is then advocated by the chief sponsor in a ten-minute speech. Although such Bills are rarely enacted, because they lack Government support, they focus Parliamentary and public attention on a particular issue. The Bill offered to me proposed a Commission to examine the problems of disabled people. It was prepared by David Owen, who had just been appointed a Minister; knowing my interest he suggested I should present it. This was just a few weeks after my return and I had not yet spoken in the Chamber.

A traditional ritual has to be followed in the presentation of such a Bill. When the proposer has made his speech, he is asked by the

Speaker for the names of the sponsors; he announces these, then he goes to the Bar of the House and bows, walks three paces and bows again. He hands a copy of the Bill to the Speaker, who formally invites him to state when the Bill will next be discussed. The standard reply of 'tomorrow' indicates an indeterminate date in the future but it is part of the ritual.

I was delighted with the opportunity but there were hazards to be faced. If I missed any of the questions, or made an error of procedure, it would be difficult for anyone to correct me on such a formal occasion. Another problem was my voice. As I was totally deaf to sound of any kind I was unable to hear my own voice and it was sometimes difficult to control the volume. The tendency was to shout—perhaps a subconscious effort to hear what I was saying—and when I did so the modulation and pitch could be adversely affected. But lowering my voice sometimes made it inaudible. When I spoke I did so from memory and the only guidance was the delicate vibration of my throat muscles. At that time this was inadequate and my clearest indication of shouting occurred when people beyond my own circle suddenly looked across.

These were some of the thoughts in my mind as I prepared my speech about the disabled. Their problems had long been close to my heart and now by an odd irony of fate I was one of them. The weekend before I was to present the Bill in the Commons there was a rally of the disabled in Trafalgar Square; hundreds of people in wheelchairs or on stretchers made it one of the most moving demonstrations I had ever attended. They had travelled from all parts of Britain and for most of them, because of their disability, the journey had been an ordeal. Relations and friends had to wheel or carry them to the demonstration, yet in the bright sunshine of Trafalgar Square there was a determined and friendly atmosphere as they formulated modest and reasonable demands for a disability income.

I was struck by the spirited way they tried to overcome their handicaps; even simple actions which most people take for granted, like drinking a cup of tea, required an elaborate and contorted performance from some of them. As I was leaving after the demonstration I saw a paralysed old man on a stretcher being lifted by two friends into an ancient van. He was helpless, yet he was joking with them as they carried him. The plight and courage of these people, so totally dependent on others, moved me and gave me a sense of perspective. I had been feeling anxious about my own performance in the House of Commons a day or two later, but their example showed me the need to forget my own problems and state an effective and persuasive case on their behalf.

The day I was to present the Bill I arranged to meet a fellow Member, Eric Ogden, in the empty Chamber before the House sat at 2.30 p.m. I explained the problem I might have with my voice. In the Chamber, while Eric sat nearby, within my range of vision, we arranged and practised a series of unostentatious signals. If my voice was satisfactory he would sit still and upright with his hands on his lap. If I spoke too loudly he would raise his hand to his face and rest his chin on it, whereas if my voice was too quiet he would lean forward attentively. No one would notice these natural movements but they would provide important guidance for me. When we had completed and rehearsed these arrangements I waited with mounting anxiety for the summons to speak. Pauline went to the visitors' gallery with Jean and Peter Thorpe, who had done so much to help me learn lip-reading.

The House was full, as is usual at the end of Question Time; Members who are not interested in a particular Ten-Minute-Rule Bill, or who have other engagements, generally leave immediately at 3.30 p.m. This is no mark of disrespect to anyone but simply the way the Commons usually works. But on this occasion, as I rose to speak, nearly everyone remained in their seats, including the Prime Minister and the Leader of the Opposition.

As the minutes ticked by I knew I was winning the House. I told them of the Trafalgar Square demonstration and what it meant to the disabled. The bleak, impersonal word 'disablement' was a synonym for personal and family tragedy, and I tried to explain the need for urgent assistance, pointing out that the disabled had no powerful trade union or pressure group to fight for them. As I moved from specific examples to the national problem and so on to international comparisons, I occasionally glanced at Eric Ogden. Not moving a muscle, he sat like a statue, eyes on me, hands in his lap. The Prime Minister looked up at Pauline in the gallery and smiled his approval at her. Well before the end I knew that the House was with me and I lost my fears. As I sat down I could sense the cheers although I could not hear them; then the Speaker rose to ask for the names of the sponsors of the Bill, which I read aloud before moving to the Bar of the House. From there, I walked in the traditional manner through the Chamber to the Speaker's Chair and on my way I passed the Prime Minister sitting near the Despatch Box. He touched my arm and I lip-read, 'Well done, Jack'. I was conscious of Pauline watching, and I was delighted that she was sharing this moment.

We went out into the sunshine on the terrace with our friends Jean and Peter Thorpe. As we enjoyed a celebration drink, Members from all parties crowded over, offering congratulations. In the excitement, I found it difficult to lip-read, but it did not matter. I had returned to the House of Commons without any hearing and my first speech in the Chamber had been warmly accepted. It was a significant day and, in its own way, a landmark; to my knowledge it was the first speech by a totally deaf man in any legislature in the world. For me it was also a happy day. I was in the company of those who understood and had helped me to return; I noticed that the Thames no longer looked bleak and cold but seemed to reflect a new sparkle in the air.

15

Friends—or Acquaintances?

I lost none of my friends when I became deaf; but it was not until I was deaf that I knew who were my friends. I learned to recognise, especially in the early days, the signs of subtly changed relationships. The middle distance acquired a new fascination for some men who gazed at it as they passed. Others hastily became aware of a sense of time, even urgency, for other appointments. Faces, formerly friendly, acquired frowns as people became suddenly preoccupied with solemn innermost thoughts. The natural expressions of others turned into forced smiles—a prelude to hail and farewell.

Inevitably, as relationships were impaired, I was repeatedly wounded by the double-edged blade of misunderstanding others and others misunderstanding me. Lack of imagination led some people to feel superior, occasionally in curious ways. One friend who had no pretensions to deep political thinking had—on the rare occasions when we discussed Parliamentary affairs—always treated my views with great respect. But now that I was deaf, this reticent, gentle man became a lion in debate. His new dogmatism was no more than a bubble of superiority, a feeling that a man short of one sense must be short of sense in general; it was amusing but it was essential to prick the bubble. Having done that I could again enjoy his genuinely pleasant companionship.

Of course the value of true friends, especially in time of need, cannot be measured. In addition to the Parliamentary friends mentioned earlier, I relied on a small group of people who accepted my disability and had an obvious desire to help me to overcome it. They needed patience and I needed persistence, because conversation was never easy in the early days of deafness.

My mother and sisters were willing to give everything they had— time, patience, understanding and love. We had always been close and they did all they could to help. With them, I always felt the pressures slipping away and even in those early days glimpsed a spark of optimism about my future.

In Widnes I always enjoyed seeing old friends like Ken and Nancy Merrifield and Jim and Ann Roach. Both the men had been shop stewards when I was the Union chairman years ago and they and their wives had become close friends over many years. Soon after I went deaf I arranged to meet Ken and Jim together one afternoon. I need not have worried about understanding them: 'How can we help, Jack?' were their first words. They had no interest in the middle distance, their watches or solemn innermost thoughts; over a drink I relaxed as we chatted about old times and put new problems into perspective. I knew that they were aghast when I became deaf because they were aware of my political aspirations and understood my deep commitment. They probably wondered how I would react to the blow and were clearly relieved when they found I was recovering my spirits and fighting on.

Another Widnes friend, Dick Topping, a tough factory worker of great sensitivity and understanding, had helped in my housing campaign in Widnes. We sometimes went hiking together, spending long weekends camping in the Lake District. Despite my deafness, we went again and his encouragement and clarity of speech greatly helped me at that time. After nightfall it was almost impossible to lip-read by torchlight; when the lights were out there was no conversation at all. But at our usual site near Bowness we spent a weekend as enjoyable as any we ever had. We trekked over the hills, talking together, conscious of the difficulties but confident that they would not affect the friendship; indeed if possible they deepened it. One mellow October evening we sat watching the sun spray a golden backcloth on the peaks. We drank a glass of beer and chatted about our early days in the slums of Widnes, contrasting those conditions with the beauty around us. It was a happy time of deep companionship and mutual understanding.

Another memorable evening, of a very different kind, occurred during those first few months. Our friends and neighbours, Peter and Jean Thorpe, who had spent so much time and effort helping me to learn lip-reading, felt it was time we had an evening out together. It was shortly after I went deaf, when I was in the midst of the exhausting discipline of a crash course in lip-reading. I had not been out to dinner since leaving hospital and I wondered how the evening would go. They took us to a small Chinese restaurant. The result was not only a happy evening but a great psychological lift at a time when I needed it most.

One of my close friends, Campbell Fraser, struck exactly the right note by helping me and then treating deafness as an irrelevance while we discussed the issues of the day or enjoyed whatever we were doing. It did not seem to matter to him whether we were talking alone or in a crowd. He spoke with great clarity, repeating sentences when necessary as if it was the most natural thing in the world.

Another friend, Phil Connell, had a similar attitude. He tried to speak clearly and although I could not easily understand him he repeated sentences as an ordinary and necessary part of our conversation; he told me that when he mentioned our talks to his wife Joan, who had given much of her time to helping me with lip-reading, he remembered the content of our discussions rather than the difficulties of lip-reading; it was a subtle and encouraging comment.

Small actions showed large hearts. When we arrived for dinner with old friends, Sir Frederick Catherwood and his wife, Elizabeth, soon after I returned from hospital, they were both well equipped with pen and paper in case I had difficulty in lip-reading. Other friends, Roy and Joy Marsh, were masters of the gentle and courteous art of blaming their speech for my lip-reading failings. My secretary Verity Turrell, experienced in deafness through her deaf son, would shake misunderstanding aside with a flick of her head, and willingly repeat a sentence when necessary.

Unfortunately not every friendship was to emerge as strong and unscathed. While I was Michael Stewart's Parliamentary Private Secretary I had become friendly with a senior Civil Servant, a man of great intellect, whose general views coincided with my own. Working fairly closely together, our friendship developed and we occasionally lunched and discussed common problems. He was one of the first to write after I became deaf and he was kind enough to invite us to lunch, in a small French restaurant in Soho. Within moments of our meeting I realised that his speech was absolutely incomprehensible to me because, although he had a good voice, his lips hardly moved. He was one of those rare people who through no fault of their own are beyond the skill of even the most expert lip-reader. Every word he spoke had to be translated for me by Pauline, from the aperitifs, right through lunch, and over coffee. It must have been a distressing experience for him and it left me very depressed.

I did not see him again until some years afterwards, when we met in a corridor of the House of Commons. He was friendly and genuinely regretted that we had not seen each other, although I am afraid he still had to convey this information through notes. Even though my lip-reading had improved, his speech was still incomprehensible to me. Although we provisionally arranged another lunch, I have never heard from him since and, of course, I don't blame him. Such is the threat of deafness to relationships, even when really genuine friends are concerned, if I am unable to lip-read them adequately.

But it was my family who provided the foundation for my climb back to normality. While I lost erstwhile friends, Pauline stood at my side; not for her the desertion of a sinking ship. The greater the difficulty the greater her efforts. She gave not only unbounded affection, but practical help with lip-reading for many weary months. The clarity of her speech made the difficult art of lip-reading relatively easy in practice. Our daughters, Jacqueline and Jane, readily understood the problems and willingly helped to solve them. Their speech was clear to me but if I encountered a difficult sentence they would find an alternative form of words I could easily understand. Through their patience I could converse as naturally, and almost as easily, as a man who could hear.

At first Caroline was too young to understand, but as she grew older she insisted on participating when I was practising lip-reading with the family. At the ripe old age of five she had a delightfully developed sense of humour and soon discovered a new way of pulling my leg. She would say something I could not understand, so I would ask her to repeat it. With a twinkle in her eye, she would do so and, if I still could not understand, she repeated it. When this had happened half a dozen times I called Jacqueline and Jane to interpret; they told me she was talking complete gobbledegook, and was greatly amused by my attempts to lip-read. It may seem odd to the outsider, but this provoked highly infectious family laughter, although I quickly learned to keep a sharp eye open for repeat performances.

Caroline has grown up with my deafness and accepts it as natural. I have learned not to try bluffing her because on occasion, when I have failed to lip-read her and pretended to understand, she has asked with impish innocence 'What did I say?' It is not often one can learn from a five-year-old, but she has taught me that it is a dangerous game pretending to understand people because it can be exposed so easily. Pauline's mother and sister, Barbara, also enjoyed her humour, although they themselves spoke clearly and naturally.

They were not inhibited by deafness and our conversation was never affected by it.

Outside the family it was naturally easier for people to speak to others with normal hearing than to a deaf person, and all too often I watched a conversational pattern emerge and repeat itself. When I was talking with one person we would get along reasonably well, depending on the attitude and intelligence of the other person and my lip-reading ability. But if anyone joined us I would gradually be squeezed out of the conversation as the other two talked to each other. No unpleasantness was involved, but it was natural for them to react to each other's comments rather than break the flow to explain things to me. In every such situation I had to decide whether to stay out of the conversation and follow as best I could, or try to intervene and exert a gentle pressure to keep it within my range of understanding. This meant interrupting, and asking one of them to repeat a sentence—something I did very sparingly. With Pauline present I could always rely on her to give me the gist of a conversation but her presence was not an unmixed blessing. People would almost invariably turn away from me and rely on her to act as interpreter. As my lip-reading improved it was sometimes better to be without her, because people were then forced to make an effort to talk directly to me; then they would discover it was not so difficult to communicate. Pauline used to pull my leg about her being indispensable in the early days but a hindrance later on.

Although discussion in groups was not easy, large dinner parties, curiously enough, were less of a problem because conversation was usually tête-à-tête. There were, however, other difficulties, as I found at an official dinner at the Mansion House in London for hundreds of aural consultants, who had been attending an international conference. I sat next to one of the wives, adjusting my voice to a fairly high level to be heard above the sound of the orchestra. At one stage everyone stood up for the National Anthem; as it finished, in a moment of levity I turned to my companion and asked 'Which anthem was that?' All around the hall people turned to look at me and I realised too late that I had failed to adjust my voice; it must have sounded as if I was using a megaphone in the relative silence following the music.

I was learning the hard way about the embarrassing traps the deaf find so difficult to avoid. They occurred in the most unexpected places. At parties when the lights were shaded to create an intimate atmosphere I would find it too dark for conversation. Such lighting, visually attractive to a person who can hear and converse freely, made my problem of lip-reading almost impossible; I would debate with myself whether to leave, flounder, or ask the host to turn the lights up. Usually I said nothing, but Pauline would invariably take the initiative and ask for better lighting if we were among friends. At official functions, of course, we had to accept the situation, but even at semi-private affairs I sensed a reluctance to spoil the atmosphere by raising the lights. At one political party, Pauline asked the hostess to lighten a darkly shaded room and although she agreed I felt uneasy. We left fairly early and before we were ten yards from the house we were amused to see the main lights go out.

Few of the general public know how to deal with total deafness. When I went shopping or travelling, I had to explain that I was deaf and relied on lip-reading. If I was unable to follow I would ask people to speak more clearly. This happened frequently at first and, if I still could not understand, I had to proffer a pencil and paper. Naturally this sometimes created irritation, particularly if people were in a hurry, but a few were embarrassed and simply shook their heads with astonishment. The majority of people did not know how to react—a railway porter talked to me with a cigarette in his mouth —but I found a surprisingly large minority automatically said 'I'm sorry', then spoke more slowly and clearly. The difficulties were not insuperable, because often the conversation was predictable and problems were mostly caused by poor speakers or bad lighting. I learned to assess accurately, within seconds of telling people I was deaf, what their reaction was going to be. Some betrayed their feelings with a sudden change of expression, a flicker of eyelids or a glint in their eyes; others smiled and took the problem in their stride. I learned to react accordingly.

Most people are more concerned about the difficulties deafness creates for them rather than the difficulties confronting the deaf. This could not have been expressed more succinctly nor innocently than by one of my Parliamentary colleagues when discussing my return to the House with me some time afterwards. He said, 'It was very difficult for *us* because we were more embarrassed than you were.' How little he knew, and how revealing his comment. At least it proved I had successfully masked my own discomfort. In striking contrast was the remark made by Harold Evans, the Editor of the *Sunday Times*, when we were discussing an article I was to write for his newspaper. Until I had grasped the pattern of his lip-movement I had a little difficulty in following him and I apologised a few times. His reaction was, 'Don't apologise—it is far more difficult for you to lip-read than it is for me to repeat things.' His comment showed an uncommon degree of comprehension.

When I first lost my hearing and some of my relationships were transformed, I felt as if I was living in a twilight world. Deafness seemed a badge of shame. Rejection by some people was the more traumatic for being sudden. Yet it was of little consequence, for the loss of some relationships can be as useful to a man as shedding fat is to an athlete. Ultimately we rely on the love of our families and the affection of our friends.

16

The World of the Deaf

When I returned to the House of Commons I did not delude myself that I could resume full political activities immediately, but I slowly increased my Parliamentary work. It would take time. Meanwhile I needed a commitment to fill the enforced gap in my life. At that time Helen Keller, the famous deaf/blind woman who had triumphed over her dual disability, died. There was some discussion in the newspapers about a possible Helen Keller Memorial Fund, and some argument about whether the deaf or the blind were entitled to the proceeds. I decided to try to bring the deaf and the blind of Britain together in the hope of establishing a joint fund to help them both.

The General Secretary at the Royal National Institute for the Deaf was helpful and anxious that the venture should succeed. But he did not seem optimistic and I did not press him to explain his reservations. When I went to the Royal National Institute for the Blind I understood his pessimism. The building was far more impressive than that of the Institute for the Deaf and it was much better staffed; although by no means lavish, it was clearly better endowed. The General Secretary was pleasant, brisk and willing to consider any initiatives and attend exploratory meetings for a joint fund; but whereas the officials for the deaf strongly supported my provisional plan, those of the blind were not notably enthusiastic. The message was conveyed tactfully, discreetly, even kindly, but it was made clear that the blind had their own ideas for raising money. It was obvious to me that any concept of a new fund to help the deaf *and* the blind was stillborn. No one had rejected the idea out of hand but the relative financial strength of the two bodies was so disparate that it indicated a long-standing difference between them. I learned later that the blind have charitable donations of some £2,000,000 a year compared with £20,000 for the deaf. With public generosity biased to this extent, I began to understand why the blind chose to avoid cooperating with the deaf.

The poverty of the organisation for the deaf is a reflection of the striking difference in the public attitude to the two disabilities. The average person feels gratified helping a blind man across the road; he feels he has done his good deed for the day. But co-operation with the deaf involves positive and continuous help rather than a gesture which is soon over and done with. No comedian would ever win a cheap laugh about the misfortunes of a blind man, but the deaf are a source of endless amusement. Equating the deaf with the daft is not confined to music halls; the public readily assume that one malady is synonymous with another. Thus they strike at people already stricken.

This may be due to a general inability to identify with the deaf. The deaf man looks normal. It requires imagination to appreciate his difficulty and it is impossible to simulate it. The eyes can be closed but the ears cannot; even when not listening, the ears hear and the brain sorts and sifts sounds. It is not surprising that the first reaction to a totally deaf man is often surprise, turning into embarrassment. Though many people try shouting, the only way they can be understood is by speaking clearly; some are willing to try, but others prefer to face the other man's problem with a stiff upper lip. Deafness requires from those who can hear a degree of patience and understanding which is in limited supply and which many people tend to reserve for their own emotional and dramatic crises.

Few people appreciate the crucial difference between the totally deaf and those who are merely hard of hearing. The hard of hearing, still able to use their ears, usually benefit from a hearing aid. They can also be helped by people speaking a little more loudly and clearly. Volume is irrelevant to the totally deaf. Many people unthinkingly shout at them, but they depend entirely on their eyes, requiring clearly enunciated speech visible on the lips.

Most deaf people are devastated by their problems, as I discovered from a vast flow of letters. Because of my growing involvement in deafness I was asked to open the biennial conference of the Royal National Institute for the Deaf in Edinburgh. I was doubtful about doing this because I was not an expert in the field, only one of the afflicted. But the letters had a great influence on me. The first public statement I made after my loss of hearing had been that I hoped to come to terms with the problems and reduce deafness to a minor irritation. This was a brave but foolhardy comment which annoyed some people with long experience of the disability. They knew how profound and far-reaching its effects can be and rightly felt I had minimised them. Deafness is the most misunderstood disability of all, and in those days I too misunderstood it.

Eventually I agreed to open the conference in Edinburgh. This was my first meeting with people actively, and in some cases professionally, concerned with deafness. I was given a warm welcome and it was clear that although the delegates regretted my personal misfortune they were delighted to have a spokesman in the House of Commons. I was a little anxious about my voice while using a microphone, as this was my first major speech to a large audience since I became deaf. But as it turned out, I had little need to worry. I spoke of the inability of the deaf to accept deafness in the way that other people accept their disabilities. Self-conscious, almost ashamed, the deaf suffer a loss of self-confidence and an increasing embarrassment which can destroy relationships already seriously impaired. I called for a transformation of public opinion from one of uncommitted indifference to one of active co-operation. Since medical science was floundering in this complex subject, I also suggested an international symposium to plan a coherent strategy of research.

The conference left me in no doubt that deaf people are commonly regarded as second-class citizens and I saw enough to convince me that they needed all the champions they could find. Most delegates complained of a public attitude of indifference, lack of resources, shortage of money and inadequate facilities. Few of them even thought it worth discussing the possibility of improvements in medical research.

Despite the warmth of my reception I had a miserable time in Edinburgh because the head noises I suffer from were exceptionally bad. Tinnitus—the thundering and roaring which affected me in the Liverpool hospital—has plagued me ever since. In the years since I became deaf I estimate that I have had no more than thirty-six waking hours free of this terrible affliction, although sometimes it is more endurable than others. When it is at its worst I try throwing myself violently into work and if that fails I take sedatives and try to find the oblivion of sleep. If, as sometimes happens, the racket persists, there is no alternative but to accept the doctor's banal advice and 'learn to live with it', although it can be as great a burden as deafness itself. Many deaf people suffer from tinnitus. Too many complacent aural consultants regretfully shrug their shoulders and offer useless advice. A cause of such suffering in other fields of medicine would attract massive and expensive research. Why not in the realm of deafness?

The opportunity to discuss this and other questions arose when I was invited to address the Otological Section of the Royal Society of Medicine in Wimpole Street. It proved to be a deeply disappointing occasion since they seemed less interested in research into nerve deafness than in the more simple hearing problems. I was dismayed at the lack of interest in the terrible problem of tinnitus. Their knowledge of it was slight; one surgeon asked my advice on what he should tell patients who suffered from tinnitus. But he was supposed to be the consultant.

There are two basic forms of deafness, conductive and perceptive —or nerve-deafness. Conductive deafness rarely presents insoluble problems because it is caused by a loss of flexibility in a chain of tiny bones in the ear which conducts sound from the eardrum to the nerve of the ear; an operation can loosen these three bones or even replace them with plastic. Even if this cannot be done, a hearing aid can largely overcome the problem. It is impossible to cure perceptive deafness because when the nerves have died there is no way of resuscitating them. The hearing loss is irreversible and when it is total, no hearing aid can help. Nerve deafness, referred to by the experts as 'sensorineural hearing loss', is the Everest of deafness, yet to be scaled by surgeons still plodding around in the foothills. The fundamental problems have not been given the time or the attention they deserve, and surgeons in this country and abroad devote a disproportionate amount of time to the lesser difficulties of conductive deafness—which seems to me suspiciously like taking the line of least resistance.

I was surprised to find that otologists have not even established the medical pattern common to most specialities in which physicians diagnose and surgeons operate. Ear surgeons do it all themselves. I thought I would try to set up an international symposium of leading ear specialists to survey existing knowledge and recommend plans for the future. Dr Ronald Hinchcliffe, one of Britain's leading research workers, gave valuable co-operation and support.

I approached the Ciba Foundation, a progressive organisation which holds regular high-level medical conferences, and asked the Director, Dr Gordon Wolstenholme, if one on hearing research was possible. He felt unable to help because of other commitments. The answer was disappointing but not shattering, because it was only my first attempt to win support for the idea. I replied that I appreciated the difficulties but I asked Dr Wolstenholme if, with his experience, he would kindly estimate for me the cost of a three-day symposium which would include about twenty specialists from Western Europe, the Middle East and the United States. I then intended to approach other organisations. To my delight, he said the Foundation had had second thoughts and were willing to organise and finance an international symposium on nerve deafness.

Later that year, in December 1969, a group of some twenty internationally distinguished otologists and neurologists attended the three-day symposium in London. The dialogue was of an exceptionally high standard—although at times incomprehensibly technical to me—and it included a full exchange of views. Disappointingly, the discussions underlined the intractability of nerve deafness. Transplantation was out of the question at the present time and although the electrical stimulation of the hearing nerve was mentioned no one was optimistic about it. The clearest message to emerge was the need for men of high quality to interest themselves in the subject and apply their minds to it. No firm plans were made and it was unreasonable to ask for them because each person was there as an individual. Nevertheless the discussions, and the relationships between the experts, may have laid the foundation for future advances. A report of the conference, subsequently published and distributed throughout the world, was highly informative and will have stimulated interest in the hitherto insoluble problem of nerve deafness.

But it is painfully evident that there is no research going on in the 1970s that will quickly solve nerve deafness. Until the foundations are laid there will be no hope for future generations of the deaf. Totally deaf children face a bleak future unless genuine progress is made. I have mentioned my secretary, Verity Turrell, who has a son deaf from birth, and I know of the problems both have faced. Their courage and persistence, like that of so many deaf children and their parents, deserve a better reward than the inadequate provisions for the deaf today. I wanted to see that the deaf—and indeed all the disabled—were not as neglected in the future as in the past. It was with these considerations in mind that I intensified my efforts in the House of Commons.

17

Working in Silence

Many political opportunities vanished when I became deaf. Ministerial office was out of the question and my back bench duties became more difficult. But it was no use bemoaning political amputation. I had to seek other means of making a constructive contribution. It was a process that could not be rushed. Fortunately my other faculties were unimpaired and in some ways they became sharper, more finely attuned, and better able to bear the heavier burden imposed on them. The important question was how well I could manage to carry out my political duties in the constituency and Westminster, despite deafness.

It affected my constituency work much less than I expected. At my regular 'surgeries' people were willing to speak clearly as they explained their problems; some even came with explanatory notes. I appreciated this although in fact I usually understood them by lip-reading, supplemented, in particularly difficult cases, by glancing at Pauline's notes. On occasions away from the 'surgery', when I could not see people's lips so clearly, it was more difficult. At one time, when some constituents were angered by the National Coal Board's refusal to accept liability for subsidence damage, I visited their homes. I had no difficulty in understanding them until they turned to the cracked foundations or broken walls they were describing. Then, if I took my eyes away from their lips to where they were pointing, I immediately lost touch with their train of thought. On the other hand, if I continued to look at them as they spoke, they were baffled. I developed a facility for selecting any part of their explanation which was repetitive to glance at the building, knowing that if I missed anything of importance Pauline would point it out to me at the appropriate time.

Although the houses were badly damaged, the Coal Board persisted in their refusal to accept liability; I was equally determined in pressing them to accept it. After reading the relevant Act, I discovered that it was the responsibility of the Board to prove they were not liable for subsidence damage; contrary to the usual canons of British justice, they were guilty until they proved their innocence.

Armed with this legal knowledge I persuaded the Chairman, Lord Robens, to pay for an independent survey by a Professor of Mining Engineering. We agreed on an independent consultant who made a careful investigation, but to my disappointment he supported the Coal Board's denial of responsibility. I lost the case but won many friends; constituents were warmly appreciative of my efforts.

People were usually grateful but, of course, there were exceptions. When one old man wanted the bus stop near his house moved I took up his case with the City Council but they rejected his request. The old man urged me to press them again. As a result the Council officials made further enquiries, took measurements and discussed all aspects of the problem at various meetings; finally they came to the conclusion that moving the bus stop to any other position would inconvenience a far greater number of people. When I told the old man his irascible rejoinder was, 'A bloody fine MP you are—can't even get a bus stop moved.'

Deafness hardly affected meetings I attended, although at first people were reluctant to ask questions in case I could not understand them. This was soon overcome when they found I could follow them by lip-reading or glancing at Pauline's notes if necessary and I rarely missed a question or failed to answer immediately the person had sat down. If it happened and I had to pause while glancing at Pauline's notes I would criticise her writing as the reason for the delay. Once people laughed the difficulties were over.

Occasionally I found my disability was a positive advantage. At one meeting where I was asked to speak about disablement I expected about a dozen to attend but when I arrived the large hall was packed with several hundred disabled people, their relatives and friends. They were anxious to listen and eager to question. It was a good meeting because we were all involved in disablement and they were conscious of my active interest in their problems.

At these meetings the signals Pauline gave me improved with time; within a few months they were practically imperceptible to other people. When I was being asked questions an apparently natural inclination of her head indicated where I should look for the speaker. The signals I gave her became similarly refined. If I needed a note which she was not making, I would quickly glance at her writing pad while trying to lip-read and immediately the words were being written for me. If I was concentrating on lip-reading when she got to the end of a page she would keep the page in a convenient position for me until I gave her a signal. At first I would mutter that I had read it, but this developed into a nod and finally a single blink which meant I did not need the note or I had already read it.

Soon after I went deaf we perfected a system for the telephone which enables me to have almost normal conversations; some callers do not even realise I am deaf. While I use the ordinary handset, Pauline listens on an additional earpiece. She simultaneously and silently repeats the caller's words, while I lip-read her; our technique has become so good that generally there is little or no pause between the end of the caller's words and my reply. Jacqueline and Jane, who have learned their mother's system, also assist me with great proficiency. Even Caroline, ever insistent to play her part, has acted as my telephone intermediary—although her contributions are reserved for more domestic conversations.

A political activity which has been surprisingly unaffected by deafness is broadcasting. I appeared frequently on radio and television before I was deaf but I expected no further invitations afterwards. However the great interest shown in my return as a deaf Member has resulted in my making many broadcasts about this and other problems connected with disablement. They have given me, and producers, confidence that my disability is no real barrier to broadcasting. I have been assisted by interviewers who speak clearly for me and, as many programmes are recorded, errors can be edited out before transmission. Naturally the harsh lighting and tension of television studios do nothing to help lip-reading but as my confidence grew I became more relaxed and agreed to live television interviews, providing I was given some idea of the questions beforehand, although I always emphasised that this in no way precluded tough or difficult questions.

In my first live television programme I had previously agreed on a line of questioning with the interviewer, who intended to ask how I managed in the House of Commons. After explaining that I sat at the end of the front bench so that I could swivel round to see both sides of the House, I waited for the next agreed question. Instead, his lips flickered twice and he looked at me enquiringly. Not understanding, I asked him to repeat his question but when he did so I still could not make sense of it. I was conscious that millions of viewers were watching as I concentrated on his meaningless lips—nothing could be edited out. I was about to admit that I was totally baffled when at the last split second it dawned on me that he was saying 'Bessie Braddock's?'. I had told him before the programme that Bessie Braddock had given me her seat at the end of the bench and he was merely inviting me to confirm this. Because I had not anticipated it, and names are always difficult to lip-read, the episode nearly ended in disaster.

I was particularly pleased to appear in the BBC's *News Review*, a unique television programme intended primarily for the deaf while still being of interest to other people. It reviews filmed news of the week, brings it up to date and includes items of special interest to deaf viewers. Announcers always speak clearly and their voices are supplemented by extensive use of captions. The editor, Bill Northwood, who takes a deep personal interest in the problems of deaf people, pioneered this new form of news presentation, which has done much to improve public understanding of deafness.

Although deafness created far fewer difficulties in broadcasting than I expected, it remained a lurking hazard. But since it was irrelevant to writing I began to turn more to journalism than I had in the past. Of course I had some reservations. The patronising expression of the London surgeon when he scribbled the word 'journalism' as an epitaph to my political career had made an indelible impression on me. Was I, by writing, beginning to accept his second faulty judgement? It is all very well for people who don't understand the immensely complicated consequences of deafness to recommend work devoid of the strain of lip-reading. They are unconsciously suggesting the path to isolation. I was aware of this, as well as of the rapport I enjoyed with audiences, when I considered doing more writing. But ideally I needed to speak *and* write since both are necessary parts of political activity. In some ways, newspaper articles can have a greater effect than speeches in the House because a backbencher's speeches are rarely reported in detail. In fact a backbench MP is lucky if he gets more than a couple of paragraphs in the national Press and he often speaks to a relatively empty House after frontbenchers have finished. Public opinion is a powerful weapon and I reached for it by writing, mainly about disablement, in such diverse newspapers as the *Sunday Times*, the *News of the World*, the *Daily Telegraph* and *Tribune*.

Nevertheless, in the final resort a Member is only as effective as his Parliamentary reputation. There is no substitute for Parliamentary work although additional interests outside the House can be valuable. I was struggling to regain my political identity, and no matter how much I broadcast or wrote it was in the House of Commons that I must ultimately succeed or fail.

I had campaigned on disablement soon after entering the House of Commons, working closely with the Disablement Income Group. Its leader, Megan du Boisson, a small, fragile woman with fine-boned delicate features, was confined to a wheelchair with multiple sclerosis. But this crippling disability in no way impaired her beauty or vitality. As a housewife who was not entitled to social security benefit, she realised how disastrous this could be for lower income families; with a friend she established the Group to fight for an appropriate income for all disabled people—as well as help with the extra expenses of disability. Her courage and dedication were moving and within a few weeks of meeting her I initiated a debate on disablement in the House. So began my long association with disabled people.

On my return to the House after becoming deaf I decided to extend my efforts for the disabled because I was receiving many letters from disabled people all over the country; their difficulties were far greater than I had previously realised. I discussed them with Megan du Boisson, looking forward to many years' fruitful co-operation, but her work was to be tragically ended when she was killed in a car crash shortly afterwards. Her death was saddening but her achievements remain as a challenge to those who care about disabled people.

The problems of the disabled are so vast and complicated, so numbing, that I did not know where to start trying to help. Apart from pain and discomfort, disabled people often suffer poverty, discrimination and neglect. Their problems have to be dealt with by the Government, local authorities, the general public—and the disabled themselves. Most of them merely seek the opportunity to help themselves, to be as independent as possible, yet independence is denied to the very people who need it most. This was evident from the unemployment rate among disabled people. The national average at the time was two per cent but the rate for the registered disabled was five times as high. Some people felt this figure of ten per cent was tolerable because they thought the disabled were unfit to work; but they did not realise that only those certified capable of working were allowed on the register. I had little doubt that the Labour Minister responsible would redress this injustice as soon as possible.

Unfortunately I was wrong. The usual bromides were offered—sympathy and regret for the disabled—but the replies to my questions were evasive and unsatisfactory. When no action was taken I asked for an adjournment debate. To make sure this was not a cosy affair I made my attitude clear at the outset when I said that I did not intend to accept the reiteration of unsatisfactory answers already given to me; I proposed to challenge them, criticise the policy and invite the Government to change it.

The results: more bromides, a few platitudes, some personal compliments on the 'force and vigour' of my speech—and no action. Far from improving, the unemployment rate of disabled people got worse. Clearly the Minister, a reasonable man, could not cope with the inertia in a Ministry machine; it was a formidable obstacle requiring a strong Parliamentary force. At that time there was no such force active on behalf of disabled people but one was badly needed. So a group of Members of all the main parties banded together to form an All-Party Disablement Group. I was elected its chairman and with John Astor, a Conservative, as secretary, we began to provide a forum and act as a pressure group on behalf of disabled people. It was desperately difficult at first because very few Members were interested in the problems. Most were more concerned with the colourful, controversial political topics of the day, so we had to rely on a few Members with a long-standing interest in various aspects of disablement.

The whole scene was transformed by a lucky chance which led to the passage of an important Act of Parliament. Alfred Morris, the MP for Manchester, Wythenshawe, was abroad when the ballot for private members' Parliamentary Bills took place, but his brother Charles, the MP for another Manchester seat, put his name down. He came top of the ballot and from this stroke of good fortune emerged special legislation to help the disabled—and reinforcements to the Parliamentary campaigners.

Whoever wins the ballot is inundated with scores of pre-packed Bills, complete with briefs and even speeches. All kinds of pressure groups are active in the House, many of them fighting for worthy causes. Members inevitably are tempted to take a well-meaning Bill which has been carefully researched and prepared. But Alf Morris chose the then obscure subject of disablement, beginning with a few notes on the back of an envelope. He asked for my views and together we discussed the general lines of a comprehensive

Bill to help disabled people. Like Topsy it 'just growed', as various Members and organisations accepted Alf Morris's invitation to draw up clauses on subjects in which they were particularly interested.

The battle for the Chronically Sick and Disabled Persons Bill had begun and it turned out to be an important one. It imposed on local authorities an obligation to discover how many disabled people lived within their areas, then to provide them with necessary and appropriate services. These significant sections galvanised indolent and indifferent authorities into finding people who had long been neglected. They had to give practical assistance in homes, recreational and educational facilities as well as other important requirements, such as telephones, where necessary. New rights of access to public buildings were established opening up opportunities hitherto denied people confined to wheelchairs. And the disabled were given representation on many Advisory Committees affecting their future. These were some of the main proposals which we were to advocate in the months ahead.

The Bill was important to all of us, but two things of personal interest emerged. The first was my friendship with Alf Morris and other Members who worked on the Bill; the second was my close involvement with the passage of the Bill in the House. Alf Morris proved to be a man with quite exceptional understanding of my problem; we soon formed a warm personal relationship which I value highly. My work on the Bill also brought me into closer touch with men like John Golding, the Member for Newcastle-under-Lyme, and Lewis Carter-Jones, the Member for Eccles. We became great friends and my connection with this group more than compensated for the loss of relationships resulting from my deafness.

Members on both sides of the House established a harmonious working relationship on the Committee for the Bill and no one tried to make political capital at any stage. My involvement, entailing much more work than I had anticipated, was exactly what I needed at that time. Working on the Bill pulled me out of the isolation of deafness; it was a psychological tonic.

We reached a stage where we needed the Government's consent to special provisions for haemophiliacs at a time when Ministers were not willing to commit themselves. Alf Morris asked me if I would press the Prime Minister and I readily agreed. It was my second meeting with Harold Wilson since I became deaf, and it was in striking contrast to the first one when Pauline had been present and everything went smoothly. This time I failed in my attempts to communicate with him in a natural way.

He greeted me cordially as I entered his room; I explained that I would try to lip-read him, although it would not matter if I was unable to do so as he could make a note for me. He nodded and replied, but I could not understand him. I asked him to repeat, but he merely gestured as if to say 'Don't worry' and wrote down a friendly comment. Thus encouraged, I told him of the special problems of haemophiliacs, explaining why we needed his support; in response, he wrote another note. Halfway through the conversation—if it could be called that—I asked him to leave the notepaper alone and I would try to lip-read him. He said that what he was explaining was difficult to lip-read—which I lip-read!—and went on writing. He was motivated by kindness and consideration but for me it was a profoundly depressing experience.

By coincidence I met his wife, Mary, a few days later at a reception. I was amused to find I could lip-read her relatively easily and I told her about my abortive attempt to talk with her husband. Although she did not comment, I felt that with her impressive understanding of the problems, gentle words would be spoken in 10 Downing Street. When I met Harold Wilson some time afterwards for a further conversation he did not touch pencil or paper, speaking so clearly that I could understand him almost as well as I could his wife.

I took a special interest in some clauses of the Bill, such as one designed to establish an Institute of Hearing Research. The Government opposed this, so I re-worded it to meet their objection that such an Institute, established by the Government, would affect the independence of the Medical Research Council. My new clause provided that the Government should collate evidence for and against an Institute and present it to the Medical Research Council. If this Clause was carried there would have to be a comprehensive enquiry into hearing research by the Government. The MRC would be obliged to establish such an Institute or take other steps to ensure that adequate research was being undertaken. Either way it would benefit the deaf.

This was not very welcome, but with the assistance of Alf Morris and members of the Committee I succeeded in pushing the second draft through. I was naturally pleased, as was Laurie Pavitt, the other MP active on behalf of the deaf. Deafness has always been neglected, research is inadequate, and the inclusion of this clause was a great step forward. Although the Government was not enthusiastic about this and one or two other clauses, they went to tremendous lengths to accommodate the sponsors, helping to ensure the passage of the Bill.

After being accepted by the Commons the Bill had to be discussed in the House of Lords, and I was dismayed by the attitude of their Lordships. Lord Longford, the principal spokesman on the Bill in the Lords, strongly supported it but he and his colleagues wanted to see a number of changes made. There was nothing wrong with that, as the function of the Lords is supposedly to improve Bills coming from the Commons. But because of strong rumours of a General Election, the Commons sponsors were anxious that the Bill should be enacted as quickly as possible; if an election were called before all the stages were completed the entire Bill would be lost. Although we recognised the good intentions of the Lords we were anxious that they should not insist on risking the whole Bill for the sake of a few amendments. Some of them were unimpressed by this argument and insisted on full discussions in the Upper House.

While their Lordships pontificated we waited apprehensively for the announcement of the date of the General Election. Finally all was well, and the Bill became law on May 29th, one of the last Acts passed by the Labour Government before the 1970 General Election. It was a notable day for the disabled as well as for those of us who had worked so passionately and enthusiastically for its passage. It was also a significant day for me, since I now knew beyond doubt that I could make a contribution in Parliament despite total deafness.

18

A Vote of Confidence

For all the goodwill in my constituency and at Westminster, I was well aware that I had not been elected as a totally deaf Member of Parliament. The support for my decision to remain after I became deaf had been overwhelming, but it had yet to be tested at the polls. When the next election came, the constituency Party would have to make its decision; if my candidature was endorsed, the people of Stoke-on-Trent would have the final verdict.

In the early months of 1970 there was much speculation about the date of the General Election. Just as we had our own bookmaker in the Wellington Street of my Lancashire boyhood, so at Westminster we had Ian Mikardo, the MP for Poplar, busily taking bets on the election date. There were over 600 well-informed tipsters in the House of Commons and their advice was supplemented by newspaper opinion. The only man who refused to comment was the Prime Minister, though it was obvious that his choice really lay between June and October. Many Labour MPs felt early in the year that October was the most likely date and the odds offered by Mikardo reflected this opinion. When I met him in a corridor he quoted evens against October and 13–2 against June. I didn't know whether the precision of this six-and-a-half-to-one offer indicated anything other than a mathematical assessment of Members' opinions, but I put down a pound on each date.

Naturally I preferred to win £6·50 on a June election, but as speculation mounted I suddenly realised that an election then might mean the loss of my seat. My majority was comfortable—providing the electors could vote; but Stoke-on-Trent comes to a virtual standstill for two weeks every year when all the factories close down simultaneously for the 'Wakes Weeks' holidays. The city is deserted as thousands of families go on holiday. Postal votes are not allowed to holidaymakers, and to make matters worse, many professional people, generally regarded as Conservative supporters, take their holidays later in the year. In 1970 'Wakes' holiday fell in the last two weeks of June. At last came the official announcement of the election date: June 18. It looked as if my efforts of the last few years were to be thwarted by an odd coincidence of timing. I stood to win my bet and lose my seat.

The crucial question was how many of my supporters would be likely to spend their holidays away from home; some local people estimated that at least sixty per cent of the houses would be empty. At the bicentenary celebration of one pottery firm I asked some employers for their estimates of the number of employees likely to be absent from the city. There was no consensus, but one went so far as to say that eighty per cent of his people went away. However, as he claimed that they all went to the South of France I took comfort from his ignorance.

A formal meeting of the General Management Committee of the Stoke-on-Trent, South, Labour Party was convened to adopt me as their Parliamentary candidate. There was no opposition. The delegates, emphasising that my deafness did not worry them, showed their confidence by a unanimous vote. I appreciated their attitude more than I could tell them and their unfailing loyalty was a source of strength to me. As the other candidates emerged I surveyed the field. A lively schoolteacher with some political experience was the Conservatives' choice, while the Communist Party nominated a bricklayer who had represented them at the previous General Election. He seemed to understand the Communist Party line fairly well but was less than formidable in debate. In the previous election he had polled over 2,000 votes and, with the effect of the holidays, his candidature could prove to be a nuisance if he held his vote.

The days of well-attended public meetings were already over; the public just did not turn out. People were kept informed by the media and kept at home by television. My job was to make personal contact with the electorate and focus on issues of special interest to Stoke-on-Trent. I aimed to visit every street in the constituency, using the loudspeakers to supplement individual contacts. My election address, decorated with a family photograph and one of Harold Wilson and myself, outlined the Government's record and carried a personal message. The local Party chairman, Sir Albert Bennett, had a part-time job as a selling agent for a firm of builders and when we were considering the details in a builders' hut one Sunday afternoon we were frequently interrupted by potential customers, but he switched from political controversy to housing without a moment's hesitation. No doubt some of the customers would have been intrigued to have seen among his blueprints and plans a preview of the election address they were shortly to receive.

The poster campaign was effective more by chance than foresight. My agent was visiting the printer when some striking cards caught his eye; they were 12 inches by 8 inches in two fluorescent colours, red and yellow, and were so designed that the centre—shaped like a circular saw—could be pressed out of the frame and interchanged. With their two bright colours, they made vivid posters which were readily identified in the constituency, even when people were too far away to read the slogan 'Labour for Jack Ashley', printed in the centre.

A crisis in the campaign arose from the delay in delivering the envelopes for election addresses. This was understandable, because every constituency had placed orders when the election was announced and some were bound to be luckier than others. Some of my fellow-MPs had large stocks, so we borrowed to enable the Party helpers to keep working. But the situation became desperate as election day approached and my supply had still not arrived. My workers were held up, as were those of my colleagues who had lent us their envelopes. We hastily examined every parcel at the railway depot until we learned that the envelopes had not even been despatched from Preston, some seventy miles away.

My election agent, Peter Bayley, volunteered to go at once and collect them. I was fortunate to have him as he was a very able man, but the election came at an inopportune time for him. A parson about to join the Army, he was in the process of packing up his house and already much of his furniture had been removed. The problems of the election campaign added to these personal difficulties but he did not hesitate to set off for Preston for the missing envelopes. He hired a van which, he was told, had a diesel engine so he filled it with diesel oil. When he had gone far enough to make it a long walk back to the garage, the van stopped. It was a petrol engine. Peter was stranded. After many telephone calls he arrived back very late in Stoke-on-Trent with the envelopes, feeling less than enthusiastic about life in general and my election in particular, and I could not blame him. He had a van without petrol, a house without furniture and a candidate without hearing. The following day he had recovered his high spirits and was forecasting a 7,000 majority for me.

My tactics were to fight on the Labour Government's record, attack the Conservatives and ignore the Communists. I did not intend to give my opponents any publicity as they were unknown. My two Parliamentary colleagues in Stoke-on-Trent, John Forrester and Bob Cant, agreed that when joint invitations were extended to all candidates we would give our views and leave the Tories and the Communists to make their case independently. This resulted in a remarkable session at a local college where we were all invited to speak.

The college had accepted our proposal for separate meetings so we assumed that we would speak one day and the Conservatives and Communists on other days. When we arrived we were taken aback to see the decorated cars of our opponents; apparently we were to rotate in a series of meetings with different groups. It was a chaotic situation with Socialists, Tories, Communists and Liberals roaming through the college searching for different rooms. It was a hot June afternoon, many of the students were in shirt sleeves, as I was, and the girls were in colourful summer dresses. As the afternoon wore on they tired of politics and, understandably, began to take a greater interest in each other. Near the end it was difficult to tell who was the more exhausted—the candidates or the students. I had no real difficulty with the questions and Pauline was always ready with notes if I needed them. I suspect that the highlight of the afternoon for many of the students was Pauline's presence. As one student put it during question time, 'Never mind the politics, who's the lovely bird with you?'

The Conservatives countered our manoeuvre to avoid giving them publicity by calling a daily press conference at which my opponent, the best of the Conservative candidates, played a leading role. Every morning John Forrester, Bob Cant, Pauline and myself met representatives of the *Evening Sentinel* and Radio Stoke. We took it in turn to give the lead story while the others supplemented it with their comments. The reporters were scrupulously fair, presenting the issues extensively and accurately. It became a fascinating exercise in local electoral tactics; our opponents would try to make political capital out of one subject and we would either counter-attack or pre-empt them on another. We also had to decide whether to base our campaign on national or local issues. In the event we strove for a balance of both and the mix appeared to be successful.

During the campaign I met and talked to hundreds of people. They were mainly concerned about the cost of living and it was obvious that the result would hinge on their interpretation of the economic factors, generally called 'bread and butter' issues. Fortunately, I had surprisingly few lip-reading problems; Pauline was always nearby when I went door-to-door canvassing and if I had any difficulty she came to the rescue. People seemed to respond to the canvassing; we decorated our car, which added a touch of carnival atmosphere. A Labour Party song had been recorded to the tune of 'John Brown's Body' and it was a popular introduction to my short, sharp speeches on the loudspeaker. I enjoyed the loudspeaker because I was used to it and knew how to project my voice even though I could not hear it. During these long, sunny days people gave us a good-humoured, lively welcome and the children joined in the gaiety and excitement of the electioneering.

Although people were friendly, it was difficult to persuade them to put posters in their windows. At least it was difficult to get them to keep them there. One day, distributing the small posters, I visited row upon row of houses and was delighted to see many people put them in their windows; nearly every house in one main road displayed the brilliant fluorescent cards. An hour later, as I drove past again, nearly every one had been taken down. It was baffling; people were anxious to oblige yet they were apparently shy about displaying their political views. One notable exception was the owner of an ice-cream van who took a batch of posters and plastered them all over his van. Most business people did not want the posters, but as I did not press them I never knew whether this was because of their own views or the danger of offending their customers. But the ice-cream van loftily maintained its clear and unashamed message until the day after the election.

Throughout the campaign, a devoted group of Party workers, including some who came back from their holiday to help, worked every day in the Labour hall, on the loudspeaker or at meetings. The campaign flourished with a crackle of excitement in the air as the political bandwagon gathered momentum. I felt people were genuinely involved and enthusiastic—until the weekend before polling Thursday. Then as I drove round the city my heart sank: the Wakes Week holiday had begun and the place seemed deserted. I wondered who was listening to my political speeches or reading the carefully prepared manifestoes in a city from which all life and vitality had fled.

It was difficult to assess how many people were at home, particularly as questions on the subject produced a variety of answers.

One suggested method of establishing how many were on holiday was to count the number of houses with windows closed during the day. I was told that, as it was so warm, women who were merely out shopping would at least leave their bedroom windows open, whereas those who had gone away were almost bound to have locked them. The first count showed that over sixty per cent of the people in my strongest areas had gone off on holiday. I argued that many of them might only have gone away for the day, or that the method of calculation might be faulty. I was whistling in the wilderness.

By polling day no one had provided any positive figures about the number of absentees. The question would only be answered when the polls had closed. At a committee room I visited early in the day I asked a little anxiously about the voting flow; the woman in charge urged me not to worry. On my return in the afternoon I determined to appear cheerful, but when I bustled in with a breezy air I was faced with a disconsolate group who showed much greater anxiety at that important stage than I had in the morning.

My daughters Jacqueline and Jane and my sister Mary joined us as we redoubled our efforts. All the Party helpers were working feverishly because no one was sure how close the issue was going to be. At 9.30 p.m. my agent, Peter Bayley, estimated, after touring the polling booths, that there was a fifty per cent poll—on our calculation this meant I had won the election. Nevertheless we kept at it until the polls closed at 10 p.m., then joined a group of helpers for a cautiously optimistic drink.

Before going to the count the family went to our house for a bath and a quick meal. We were all tired but in good spirits which were not affected by the radio news just before we left. The first election result showed a swing against Labour, but we confidently assumed this was a freak result and set off for the count. We arrived to see an astonishing scene. In one large hall, where the votes of the three Stoke-on-Trent constituencies were being counted, crowds of people milled around excitedly. But they were less interested in the votes being counted than in the news coming over portable radios. Conservatives listened jubilantly and shouted the latest results to their friends while our supporters were despondent. We were dumbfounded to learn that the Labour Government was tumbling to a disastrous defeat.

I was saddened to hear that such great friends as Gordon Oakes of Bolton, West, and Evan Luard of Oxford, had lost their seats, along with many others. The Tories rejoiced, and our dismay at this startling turn of events obviously showed in our faces; I was suddenly aware that it must be upsetting Jacqueline and Jane, who were watching from the gallery and awaiting my result. They had, in fact, assumed from the expressions of Labour and Conservative officials in the counting hall that I had lost the election. I signalled to them as soon as possible that I had won. The people of Stoke-on-Trent had given me a heart-warming endorsement, with an electoral swing against me less than the national average swing against the Labour Party.

Next day BBC television invited me to appear on their special election programme which had been covering the campaign since it started; in this final edition the results were analysed and some of the contestants interviewed. I was asked to go to the Birmingham studios and there I sat in the same chair as Edward Heath had sat despondently a few days earlier. Now he was Prime Minister. An old friend, Robin Day, who was the interviewer in London, gave me prior notice of the questions he was to ask, in case I had difficulty lip-reading him on the screen. They were mainly about my own campaign and the way I had handled the problems of deafness. When we were on the air he made no attempt to obscure my difficulties; in fact he told viewers he intended to signal the number of each question to me and he did so with his fingers. No danger of misunderstanding there!

The effect of a change of government is felt throughout the country, but of course it is seen at its most dramatic when the House of Commons reassembles. Our leaders, who had occupied the Government front benches, with us behind and supporting them, were now on the Opposition side. Before the election we knew that however energetically the Opposition might state its case it was our decisions that counted and our majority that was decisive. Now the tables were turned; watching our opponents occupy the Government side of the House we had to accept that their decisions and their majority were now paramount, no matter how hard we fought. It was a difficult transition for both sides to make and more than one Government supporter was seen absentmindedly walking to the Opposition benches and sitting down there from sheer habit. Our side faced the greater difficulty in adapting to the new circumstances, but it was important that we should do so without remorse or recrimination.

The first business of the new House of Commons was to appoint a Speaker. The longest-serving Member on the Government benches, the 'Father of the House', Robin Turton, was invited to speak for his side and I was chosen to represent the Opposition. It was a rare honour and I appreciated being selected for such a distinguished occasion. The atmosphere was unusual, since there was no Speaker in the Chair to control a packed House. In accordance with tradition, the Chief Clerk stood and pointed to the Member selected to speak to the Motion. Robin Turton proposed the re-election of Dr Horace King in a good speech.

When my turn came I spoke of the unique nature of the Speaker's office. We were inviting an individual to be the living embodiment of the ultimate paradox of being our obedient servant and our complete master. We were offering him the highest office and the greatest responsibility for our conduct. I dwelt on the character of Dr King and the combination of strength and humanity he had displayed in office.

But there was also a political message I wanted to convey, because immigration and the Irish question were to become important topics in this new Parliament. I warned that if the witches' brew of racial hatred or religious bigotry was poured into the political cauldron the House could explode with feeling which could rock it to its foundations. I felt it was an important theme and the response I received from both sides of the House seemed to confirm it. I received many congratulations from Ministers as well as from our own side but one of the comments which I appreciated most came from Norman Shrapnel, the Parliamentary reporter of the *Guardian*, who said that it was an unusually meaningful speech for such a formal occasion.

The next few weeks were a period of readjustment for both sides of the House, with Edward Heath in the new and unfamiliar role of Prime Minister and Harold Wilson back in his former position as Leader of the Opposition. It was so difficult to adjust that some senior Ministers, including the Chancellor of the Exchequer, continued to refer unthinkingly to Harold Wilson as the Prime Minister. It may have been amusing to some Members but I am sure it was not funny to Harold Wilson. The loss of office must have been a shattering experience for him, the more so because it was unexpected. One moment he dominated a powerful government machine from 10 Downing Street, with all its resources at his disposal, and the next he was practically on his own. I saw this vividly one night when I left the Members' entrance to drive home. He was standing in a small queue waiting for a taxi. He was always considerate to others and I wanted to help, but somehow it seemed presumptuous to offer a lift to the man who had been Prime Minister a week ago.

Although I regretted our loss of office I welcomed the opportunity of attacking the Conservative Government, but I was faced with a unique personal situation. Members were considerate with me because I was deaf. Outside the Chamber the problem sorted itself out as I could laugh and joke with people and soon establish a natural relationship, but it was difficult during formal Parliamentary proceedings. If the Government and its supporters gave me excessive consideration it would appear that I was taking advantage of sympathy for my affliction when I criticised them. Yet if I was uncritical I would be failing to carry out an important aspect of the job I had been elected to do.

My dilemma was underlined by a Labour colleague who objected to a critical barrage of Parliamentary Questions I addressed to the Prime Minister. When I challenged this view he said that if I persisted the Government might withdraw its co-operation. The real issue was more subtle than that because the Government was offering me no co-operation, except to speak clearly when Ministers addressed me. What my colleague had in mind, consciously or subconsciously, was that, as I was disabled, I should keep my proper place and not get above it by attacking the Prime Minister. It was a revealing comment which unthinkingly illuminated an attitude often taken by the general public towards disabled people as a whole and deaf people in particular.

I decided to risk this misunderstanding, feeling that the House of Commons would appreciate that criticism of the Prime Minister and his colleagues was as much part of my right and duty as anyone else's. This attitude proved to be justified, because although a few other Members may have objected on similar grounds to those voiced by my colleague, I believe the House accepted that I should hit as hard as I could politically and Ministers should not pull their punches in return.

Ever since the 1970 General Election, the Prime Minister, Edward Heath, has shown a deep awareness of my problems. When I have addressed critical questions to him he has always answered in kind, but looking straight at me and speaking clearly to ease the strain of lip-reading; his attitude has been typical of the House. At first there must have been a sense of slight shock in having me there, but my disability was swiftly and quietly accepted. While I was grappling to come to terms with deafness the House of Commons unostentatiously and generously came to terms with me.

Any person without a vital faculty like hearing is bound to feel deprived and unable to fulfil himself. My hopes and aspirations have been shattered by deafness and the course of my life radically changed. At one time my future lay in pieces with little prospect of picking them up and putting them together again. Everything, from my relationships with other people to my greatest ambitions, was affected. Yet from this personal disaster there has emerged something which I would never have known had it not happened. The depths of human affection and kindness are not plumbed without a crisis. Nor is the veneer of superficial relationships removed so starkly under normal circumstances. Reserves, physical and mental, remain largely dormant until they are called upon to meet an urgent personal dilemma. Deafness has given me a profound appreciation of my family and real friends; an insight into the unrecognised humanity of the House of Commons; a knowledge of despair and hope I would never otherwise have known, and a greater understanding of my fellow men.

Index

[189]